A
LITERARY
HISTORY
OF
SPAIN

41-5

A LITERARY HISTORY OF SPAIN

General Editor: R. O. JONES
Cervantes Professor of Spanish, King's College, University of London

THE MIDDLE AGES
by A. D. DEYERMOND
Professor of Spanish, Westfield College, University of London

THE GOLDEN AGE: PROSE AND POETRY
by R. O. JONES

THE GOLDEN AGE: DRAMA
by EDWARD M. WILSON
Professor of Spanish, University of Cambridge
and DUNCAN MOIR
Lecturer in Spanish, University of Southampton

THE EIGHTEENTH CENTURY
by NIGEL GLENDINNING
Professor of Spanish, Trinity College, University of Dublin

THE NINETEENTH CENTURY
by DONALD L. SHAW
Senior Lecturer in Hispanic Studies, University of Edinburgh

THE TWENTIETH CENTURY
by G. G. BROWN
Lecturer in Spanish, Queen Mary College, University of London

SPANISH AMERICAN LITERATURE
SINCE INDEPENDENCE
by JEAN FRANCO
Professor of Latin American Literature, University of Essex

CATALAN LITERATURE
by ARTHUR TERRY
Professor of Spanish, The Queen's University, Belfast

A LITERARY HISTORY OF SPAIN

THE TWENTIETH CENTURY

A LITERARY
HISTORY OF SPAIN

THE TWENTIETH
CENTURY

G. G. BROWN

Lecturer in Spanish, Queen Mary College
University of London

LONDON · ERNEST BENN LIMITED

NEW YORK · BARNES & NOBLE INC

First published 1972 by Ernest Benn Limited
Bouverie House · Fleet Street · London · EC4A 2DL
and Barnes & Noble Inc. · 49 East 33rd Street · New York 10016
(a division of Harper & Row Publishers, Inc.)

Distributed in Canada by
The General Publishing Company Limited · Toronto

© G. G. Brown 1972

Printed in Great Britain

ISBN 0 510-32291-3

ISBN 0-389 04623-X (U.S.A.)

Paperback 0 510-32292-1

Paperback 0-389 04624-8 (U.S.A.)

FOREWORD BY THE GENERAL EDITOR

SPANISH, the language of what was in its day the greatest of European powers, became the common tongue of the most far-flung Empire the world had until then seen. Today, in number of speakers, Spanish is one of the world's major languages. The literature written in Spanish is correspondingly rich. The earliest European lyrics in a post-classical vernacular that we know of (if we except Welsh and Irish) were written in Spain; the modern novel was born there; there too was written some of the greatest European poetry and drama; and some of the most interesting works of our time are being written in Spanish.

Nevertheless, this new history may require some explanation and even justification. Our justification is that a new and up-to-date English-language history seemed called for to serve the increasing interest now being taken in Spanish. There have been other English-language histories in the past, some of them very good, but none on this scale.

Every history is a compromise between aims difficult or even impossible to reconcile. This one is no exception. While imaginative literature is our main concern, we have tried to relate that literature to the society in and for which it was written, but without subordinating criticism to amateur sociology. Since not everything could be given equal attention (even if it were desirable to do so) we have concentrated on those writers and works of manifestly outstanding artistic importance to us their modern readers, with the inevitable consequence that many interesting minor writers are reduced to names and dates, and the even lesser are often not mentioned at all. Though we have tried also to provide a usable work of general reference, we offer the history primarily as a guide to the understanding and appreciation of what we consider of greatest value in the literatures of Spain and Spanish America.

Beyond a necessary minimum, no attempt has been made to arrive at uniform criteria; the history displays therefore the variety of approach and opinion that is to be found in a good university department of literature, a variety which we hope will prove stimulating. Each section takes account of the accepted works of scholarship in its field, but we do not offer our history as a grey consensus of received opinion; each contributor has imposed his own interpretation to the extent that this could be supported with solid scholarship and argument.

Though the literature of Spanish America is not to be regarded simply as an offshoot of the literature of Spain, it seemed natural to link the two in our history since Spanish civilisation has left an indelible stamp on the Americas. Since Catalonia has been so long a part of Spain it seemed equally justified to include Catalan literature, an important influence on Spanish literature at certain times, and a highly interesting literature in its own right.

The bibliographies are not meant to be exhaustive. They are intended only as a guide to further reading. For more exhaustive inquiry recourse should be had to general bibliographies such as that by J. Simón Díaz.

R.O.J.

PREFACE

IN PREPARING AND REVISING THE PRESENT VOLUME I have been given valuable help by the General Editor, Professor R. O. Jones, by Dr J. W. Butt of King's College, London, Dr A. K. G. Paterson of Queen Mary College, London, Dr María Cruz Seoane and Don Daniel Sueiro of Madrid, and especially by my wife, María Teresa Seoane. I am extremely grateful to all of them for their kindness. I should also like to express my thanks to Queen Mary College and to Professor L. P. Harvey, Head of the Department of Spanish, for allowing me a term's leave of absence to work on this book.

G.G.B.

London
July 1971

CONTENTS

LIST OF ABBREVIATIONS

BH	Bulletin Hispanique
BHS	Bulletin of Hispanic Studies
HR	Hispanic Review
OC	G. Miro, *Obras completas* (4th edn., Madrid, 1961)
PMLA	*Publications of the Modern Language Association of America*
PSA	*Papeles de Son Armadans*
RO	*Revista de Occidente*
TA	J. R. Jiménez, *Tercera antología* (Madrid, 1957)

INTRODUCTION

SPAIN 1900–39

CONTEMPORARY TESTIMONY AND PERSONAL MEMORIES of urban life in Spain during the early part of the twentieth century often make surprised reference to the atmosphere of gay euphoria that prevailed among all social classes while the nation staggered from the disaster of 1898 through a whole series of further catastrophes. The pessimism of the writers of the so-called Generation of 1898 contrasts strangely with the general public's indefatigable pursuit of amusement and pleasure. Yet the anguish and the frivolity which equally characterise the whole period up to the Civil War can be seen as symptoms of the same malaise. It is not that society was divided into a minority of tormented intellectuals and a majority of Gadarene swine. Many writers and artists who felt that life was cruel, sordid, and meaningless, and contemporary Spanish life particularly so, reacted, like Valle-Inclán's Max Estrella or the characters of Pérez de Ayala's *Troteras y danzaderas,* with outrageous, 'bohemian' behaviour, often accompanied by a literally fatal recourse to drink, drugs, and sexual pleasure. In the first few years of the century, even to be a *modernista* meant, as far as many an honest bourgeois was concerned, to lack seriousness, to live, dress, write, or paint in an extravagant and irresponsible manner. When *modernismo* became respectable, the apparent frivolity of the arts did not end. After the First World War it seemed to some that the flood of artistic '-isms' that burst on Spain was turning art into a nonsensical hoax. Yet there are plenty of signs to suggest that a principal cause of art's tendency to stick its tongue out at life was the conviction that to take life seriously would break a man's heart. Some writers sum up the apparent paradox in their own literary personalities. Unamuno's spiritual anguish is often disconcertingly expressed in what seems to be playful jesting; Valle-Inclán's rage at the spectacle of Spanish life produced some of the most brilliantly comic writing in the language; Ramón Gómez de la

I

Serna's urge to be in the vanguard of even the most frivolous literary fashions does not conceal a vein of despair and revulsion in his attitude to life. A grotesque mixture of comic and tragic moods was nothing new to Spanish literature, but during this period particularly, if a writer promises a farce, or a children's entertainment, or similar light diversions, we may normally prepare ourselves for some grim comment on the human condition, with the possibility of some ugly violence and perhaps a suicide or two.

As always, the general mood of the period's literature can be explained up to a point by reference to historical circumstances, to the broadly philosophic assumptions characteristic of the age, and to its writers' way of understanding the function of art. As regards the first of these factors, political and social conditions in Spain throughout the period were of a kind to depress and repel anyone who seriously considered them. The intolerable social injustice which had provoked violent protest and brutal repression in the nineties did not decrease in the new century, and it pressed the great majority of writers and artists into anti-authoritarian postures. An unpopular, futile, and frequently disastrous campaign dragged on in Morocco. In the middle of the period, the European war affected neutral Spain very seriously. In the first place it divided Spanish opinion sharply into pro-Allied and pro-German camps. With very few exceptions, artists and intellectuals favoured the Allied cause, and so deepened the enmity between them and the Church, the army, businessmen, and others who felt that a German victory would make Europe a little safer from impiety, democracy, and the communism which triumphed so alarmingly in Russia in 1917. The war also caused serious economic inflation in Spain, worsening the already wretched plight of the poor, provoking more strikes and violence, and putting the fraudulent and increasingly unworkable political system of the Restoration to its last test, which it failed. From 1917 onwards the system tottered towards its final collapse, while each section of society organised itself to defend its interests against the rest, in the way described by Ortega y Gasset's *España invertebrada* of 1921. Although Ortega deplored this compartmentalisation, he was no democrat, and his solution was, in effect, that the other sectors should relinquish their conflicting interests and allow his own compartment—the intellectuals—to direct the lives of everyone. This idea had a strong and persistent attraction for Spanish writers up to and even beyond 1931. Not only essayists like Ortega and Ramiro de Maeztu, but creative writers like Unamuno and Pérez de Ayala, devoted a great deal of their energy to political activity, with the direct aim of transforming public opinion and political events, and often on the assumption that they would be the acknowledged architects of a new Spain.

Actual events naturally disappointed such expectations, both in the chaotic years 1917-23 and after 1931. The parliamentary shambles was brought to an end not by intellectuals, but by a military *coup*, and from 1923 to 1930 Spain endured the dictatorship of General Primo de Rivera. Inevitably, most writers and artists vehemently opposed his rule, and that of his accomplice, King Alfonso XIII. But as modern dictators go, Primo de Rivera was a relatively benign one, and his style of government put his intellectual opponents in a rather unusual position. While they found his tyranny odious, and for the most part committed themselves to its overthrow and the establishment of a republic, the tyrant, within certain remarkably broad limits, allowed them to say so. Sustained, outspoken abuse directed at his person sometimes stung him into making angry reprisals. Unamuno was dismissed from his Rectorship of Salamanca University and exiled to the Canaries in 1924 for his fierce attacks on the dictator. Valle-Inclán's play *La hija del capitán*, which contained savage satire of the army, was seized by the police when it appeared in 1927, and Valle-Inclán was gaoled briefly in 1929 as an attempt to teach him to behave himself. But Primo de Rivera invariably half-repented of such acts afterwards. Unamuno could have returned to Spain soon after his exile began, and could even have continued to write if he would moderate his tone; but he was not prepared to do either. Valle-Inclán was soon released, unrepentant, from prison, and permitted to resume his non-conformist ways.

More importantly for literature, where Primo de Rivera did not feel that his personal or military honour was affected, he meddled very little with the considerable artistic freedom that had existed before his *coup*. *La hija del capitán* contained insults no Spanish general could let pass, but other works by Valle-Inclán which made bitter or derisive comment on the state of Spain, her monarchy, government, and police, were allowed to appear. Furthermore, official attitudes to the control of the arts on moral or religious grounds were exceedingly permissive compared with those of the late nineteenth century or, more strikingly, of the period from 1939 to the present day, and this applied equally to imported foreign publications and native work. Priests could still forbid their flock to read dangerous books, of course, and conventional opinion could reject novels, poems, and plays as being subversive or distasteful. Such factors continued to make the lot of many serious writers a rather depressing one; but if they could find a publisher they could normally deal fairly freely with controversial subjects, and speak plainly of the indecency, in every sense, of contemporary Spanish life.

Naturally this freedom did not diminish with the coming of the Republic in 1931. But nor, unhappily, did the occasion for angry protest about the state of Spain. The older writers, like Unamuno, Ortega, and Pérez de Ayala, found that the new Spain which they felt they had worked so hard to bring into being did not look to them for leadership or guidance, and was indeed not at all the new Spain they had had in mind. They also found, once the initial joy of having achieved a peaceful transition from dictatorship to republic had worn off, that this dissatisfaction was one they shared with a great many younger Spaniards of widely different political and social persuasions. Nevertheless, the five years of republican rule were an encouraging period for Spanish literature, and when political quarrels degenerated into Civil War, it was a tragedy for the arts within the greater tragedy. Republican governments had given better support to cultural and educational projects than they had received since the reign of Charles III, and had restored or elevated to positions of official distinction writers who had spent most of their lives as rebels against official and conventional attitudes. The impressive renaissance of the arts in twentieth-century Spain showed no sign of waning during the Republic. On the contrary, many of the writers who had already given substantial evidence of great talent were still young, particularly in the field of poetry. The early thirties even saw signs of a new vigour and originality in the theatre, which had been the weakest of Spain's literary genres for many decades.

Franco's rebellion destroyed the exciting future it had seemed legitimate to expect. Some writers and thinkers escaped into exile with almost indecent haste. A number died. Others offered their intellectual and literary talents to the Republic as weapons of war, and held on until the Nationalist victory drove them into exile. Very few literary figures of any stature remained in Spain at the end of 1939. Those who resigned themselves to exile followed diverse and often lonely literary paths, so that it is no longer possible to speak of general characteristics of Spanish literature after the war if that literature is understood as including the work of many of the best living Spanish writers. Those who returned soon after the conflict ended came as furtive, muted individuals, regarded with suspicion and hostility by the victors of the war.

When serious Spaniards turned from the depressing political and social reality of Spain during this period to deeper philosophical reflection, they found little relief for their pessimism. Their immediate world was detestable, a society devoid of ideals, purpose, or direction. Those who looked abroad for better things in the early years of the century soon saw the nations which had often served as models for Spanish schemes for reform swept for no good reason into four years of dreadful carnage on a hitherto unknown scale. Foreign and native prophets of the end of Western civilisation were accorded gloomy assent throughout the period. Hope was in short supply, and few possessed even as much positive spirit as Eugenio D'Ors, who affirmed in his innumerable, elegant essays on art, history, philosophy, and politics, the need to preserve and reassert the classical values of European culture, which he saw as being chiefly intelligence, order, clarity, and craftsmanship.

More commonly, thinking men continued to see modern man's dilemma as they had seen it at the end of the nineteenth century, in the stark terms which form the core of Unamuno's *Del sentimiento trágico de la vida* of 1913: truth and consolation are incompatible. What is true is unbearable, and what offers consolation must be a lie. Intellect and sentiment make both truth and consolation deeply necessary to human beings, but if we are honest, we must recognise that the pursuit of either means the loss of the other. The Church, for example, purveys a remedy for what Unamuno regards as man's deepest need, the need not to die. But in the light of reason, the consolation it offers is false, and for a man like Unamuno, as for most of the best Spanish writers of his day, the demands of reason were as excruciatingly imperious as those of sentiment. Reason, as D'Ors put it, has its feelings of which the heart knows nothing.

The collapse of belief in traditional sources of consolation, in an ordered, purposeful universe presided over by some intelligent and possibly intelligible power or principle, had of course begun to make itself felt in Spanish writing at least a hundred years before Unamuno suffered from it. What characterises twentieth-century pessimism, and distinguishes it from that of the Romantic period, is that twentieth-century writers had witnessed another collapse: the disintegration of the optimism inspired for a while by scientific rationalism in the

second half of the nineteenth century. In this connection it is necessary to observe the plain but curious fact that the best Spanish
literature of the last three centuries has very rarely been written by
orthodox Catholics—curious because the literature of other countries
would seem to show that there is no necessary correlation between
good writing and disagreement with the Christian Church, Catholic
or Protestant. In the twentieth century, the fact becomes even less
debatable. In spite of religious yearnings like Unamuno's, all the
best literature of this age is the work of agnostics or atheists. In the
eighties and nineties of the previous century agnosticism did not have
to be pessimistic. Thinking men who could not accept the spiritual
comfort offered by the Church had often been able to find alternative
grounds for a kind of hope in the rational conquest of knowledge,
and in the widely applied and applauded concept of evolutionary
progress. But in the twentieth century the findings of reason only
added an extra dimension to despair, and the idea of progress became
a bitter mockery.

In Spain, as in other countries, the anguish of the situation provoked attempts to undermine the authority of rationalism itself.
Assaults were mounted from different positions—metaphysical,
existential, phenomenological, psychoanalytical. Rationalism was
accused of failing to get to grips with reality in a meaningful way.
The old argument that runs through Hume, Kant, and Schopenhauer
was revived: for all its success at explaining relationships between the
phenomena of experience, rationalism offers no means of ascertaining
the nature (or even the existence) of an objective reality independent
of our perceptions and the inferences we draw from them. Although
this shortcoming rarely bothers the man in the street, it can be
deeply disturbing for those who urgently wish to know the meaning
of life and death. Furthermore, rationalism ignores the fact that what
concerns us most as living individuals is not in any case the ultimate,
true nature of reality, but our relation to it.

Unamuno chooses to work from metaphysical objections towards
an existential outlook. With the help of the philosophers mentioned,
and of Kierkegaard, he argues his way to the assertion that, since
rationalism might be only intrasubjective and cannot testify to the
non-existence of non-rational reality, we are left in a state of absolute
doubt which can never be resolved. But doubt, for Unamuno, is
more fecund than certain despair, in that it leaves open an avenue
where the will to believe can operate, if only on the qualified

existential basis of an existential 'as-if' postulate. So Unamuno concludes *Del sentimiento trágico* by saying, in effect, that rationalism's inbuilt, self-destroying scepticism authorises us to construct belief, and indeed to behave, as if what we need to believe were true. Ortega's objections to rationalism are also basically of an existential kind, but, writing rather later than Unamuno, he places more emphasis on phenomenological aspects. Rationalism takes for granted the independent existence of an objective reality. With one eye on Husserl and another on Einstein, Ortega argues that by neglecting to observe that, as far as human beings are concerned, reality is always something perceived by somebody, rationalism can easily lose itself in meaningless abstraction. The act of perception therefore becomes, for Ortega, a principal and integral element of reality itself. This idea is first sketched briefly as the theory of *perspectivismo* which appears in the prologue to his early *Meditaciones del Quijote* (1914): reality is the relation of individuals to their circumstances, and the most complete and authentic reality is the largest possible combination of perspectives. Ortega then develops the theme sporadically in his voluminous writings on many subjects, often giving it highly suggestive implications when he applies it to art, but it finds its fullest expression in *El tema de nuestro tiempo* (1923). Here he adds to *perspectivismo* the concept of *razón vital*, which is no more than a commonsense compromise with the limitations of rationalism. Although rationalism, ignoring the importance of perspective, cannot claim to be a completely adequate method of knowledge, that is no reason for abandoning it, says Ortega. It remains an indispensable instrument for understanding our circumstances, and without it we should be reduced to the state of mental savages. But its findings and dictates must always be related to what Ortega calls *imperativos vitales*. When it explains something, account must be taken of what the explanation means to actual individuals. When it postulates reasonable norms of behaviour, they must be considered in the context of the reality of human instincts and impulses, desires and fears, before authority is conceded to them.

Unamuno's philosophical essays of the early years of the century, and Ortega's in the twenties and thirties, represent, in their different ways, a change in Spain's ideological climate which had important consequences for literature, and caused the writing of the period to differ radically from that of the latter part of the previous century. The reservations about rationalism's unique authority expressed by

Unamuno and Ortega were in a sense complemented by a serious interest among artists in the findings of psychoanalysts like Freud and Jung, and in the mythological studies of anthropologists like Frazer and Malinowski. Surrealism never really captured any major Spanish writer—which may be a way of saying that if it had, he would not have been a major writer—but as a stimulant and a liberating influence it had a marked effect on all literary genres in Spain.

The exact nature of the changes brought about in twentieth-century literature by twentieth-century thought will, it is hoped, emerge from the following chapters; but certain introductory generalisations may not be out of place at this point. A notable feature of literature in the early years of the century is its mood of despair, the spiritual disease to which the writers themselves gave such names as *angustia vital, angustia metafísica,* and *enfermedad del ideal,* indicating the need for, and the failure to find, anything on which to base faith, hope, or even charity. Such an outlook directly influenced both the matter and the manner of Spanish creative writing. An intense preoccupation with mortality, with the transience of things in passing time, is characteristic of the age, and is a central theme in the poetry of Antonio Machado and Juan Ramón Jiménez. It is an ancient literary topic, but it acquires a new urgency when accompanied by the existential view that for any individual, death means the end of the whole universe. Another venerable topic, that art may offer consolation or escape from reality and may supply or create some of the things that reality lacks, is also re-examined earnestly by writers of this period, for whom reality was every bit as harrowing and ugly as it had been for the Romantics. The tendency to regard art essentially as an alternative to life received added impetus, throughout the period, from another direction. The decline in prestige of the scientific rationalism which had conferred authority on literary realism in the nineteenth century was accompanied by a widespread waning of interest in representational art. This was clearly a European phenomenon which affected all the arts, and tended to reduce their appeal to a small, educated minority audience. But in Spanish literature, perhaps more than in that of other nations, this waning of interest was not reflected in readers' tastes. Indifference to the elements of anecdote and description, to telling human stories or making poetry out of common experience with which readers could easily identify, was an indifference among writers, not their public. This, as will be shown, was crucial to the development of Spanish drama in the twentieth century.

In the middle of the period, after the First World War, a third factor, this time one which has nothing to do with philosophical outlook, further encouraged the tendency away from representational art: the establishment of the cinema as a popular entertainment. Spanish writers and artists took the cinema seriously from an early date. Ortega's prestigious *Revista de Occidente*, founded in 1923, devoted considerable critical attention to it. The cinema's influence on literature took various forms, but one of them was certainly its challenge to writers to do something other than what films could do better. An idea frequently expressed in Spain during the first part of the century was that, just as the development of photography had affected nineteenth-century painting, the cinema, the new form of popular entertainment, would now make representational narrative literature redundant. On the other hand, the cinema itself did not have to be realistic, and in fact was often not so. This is true not only of the early work of sophisticated directors like Clair and Buñuel, but of the films which made the greatest impact on Spanish literature in the twenties, the silent comedies of Chaplin, Keaton, Lloyd, and the rest. The extraordinary veneration in which these actors, especially Chaplin and Keaton, were held by many Spanish writers was more than a cultish affectation. The tragic undertones of their melancholy alienation from modern society, in the midst of grotesque slapstick, appealed to Spanish taste. And the bewildering episodic fragmentation, the incongruous inconsequentiality of the action, and the jerky, accelerated, puppet-like movements and gestures of these films, seemed to many thoughtful Spaniards to reflect the absurdity of modern existence in a perfectly serious and imaginative way. Lorca and Alberti, among others, paid direct tribute to these actors in their poetry, and tried to convert the experience of their films into literature. In a more indirect way, the influence of this kind of cinema on Spanish writing has been even more important. Some of the *Revista de Occidente*'s distinguished film critics—Benjamín Jarnés, Francisco Ayala—pursued the possibility of incorporating cinematic techniques in their own creative writing. The cinema's influence is also to be observed in much of Valle-Inclán's later work. Several of the techniques of the *esperpento* clearly derive from the silent comedies, and much of his drama is better suited to the screen than to the stage. For some, then, the cinema seemed about to take over the role of the realist novel and drama, obliging literature to turn to something other than telling stories and copying life. Others paid more heed to its new, suggestive powers, not for copying life, but for interpreting it and transforming it into something different and original. The two views of the cinema are diametrically opposed, but they rest on the same assumptions about the function of literary art, which are once again that literature should be distinct from life, and should not concern itself with creating an illusion of reality. Most writers of the period—though not all—accepted that real experience should continue to supply the raw material for their art, but thought that the art itself lay in the way in which the material was treated. It may well be argued that this had never ceased to be the real nature of art; but the renewed emphasis given to the concept in the present century stands in marked contrast to the theoretically documentary approach of many nineteenth-century writers. In the twentieth century, literature, like Ortega's view of reality and Unamuno's view of its meaning, becomes pre-eminently a matter of perspective and of the content of consciousness. Poets, novelists, and dramatists are less concerned with life than with defining the response they find themselves making to it, even though that response may be a gesture of repudiation.

Such a gesture, turning away from reality in search of something less depressing and distasteful, is indeed the most characteristic response made by artists of this period. Social historians who go to creative literature for information about social history, or critics who approach literature in the spirit of social historians, will find singularly little to interest them in this age. But from another point of view, that is the greatest glory of its literature. Although it is no more and no less the product of historical circumstances than any other literature, those circumstances are abnormally unhelpful in accounting for its qualities, and above all for its excellence. The best work of this period was done by exceptionally cultivated writers of keen aesthetic sensibility. What they had read was as important to their art as what they had experienced, and they were more conscious than Spanish writers had been for three centuries of great literary traditions, ancient and modern, Spanish and foreign. Appreciation of other writing enriched their work immeasurably. The anonymous authors of the *Romancero* and of folk-poetry, the splendid literary heritage of the Golden Age, and European literature of the immediate past and the present, all provided Spanish writers of this age with fertile sources of inspiration. There was rarely any question, however, of treating tradition merely as a source of models to be copied. The first four decades of the century were a time of much ingenious and exciting literary experiment, and the writing of this period reflects a remarkable sense of artistic confidence and freedom. Not all the experiments were successful, of course, and many have not stood the test of the relatively short time that has elapsed since they were made. Unwarranted confidence and ill-used freedom produced their crop of literary contributions to the flimsy euphoria of pre-1914 Europe and the lunacies of the Jazz Age. But the prevailing atmosphere was one which encouraged genuinely talented writers to extend themselves imaginatively and to produce highly original works of great power and interest. In short, what makes the twentieth century up to the Civil War a brilliant period for Spanish letters is what ultimately constitutes the greatness of any great period of literature: a substantial number of writers whose work merits lasting recognition and elicits lasting response precisely because it defies and transcends explanation and definition in terms of the circumstances in which it was produced.

Chapter 1

THE NOVEL

THE *angustia vital* OF SPANISH WRITERS at the turn of the century found its first expression in the highly personal novels of Ganivet, Azorín, Baroja, and Pérez de Ayala,[1] episodic fictional quests through the valley of the shadow of death which convey a message of frustration and despair at ever finding a purpose or a meaning in human existence. The anguish, however, turned out to be a very fertile source of literary experiment, and of some exceptionally interesting and original writing. It was as much a philosophical as a vital anguish, and among the consequences of the collapse of confidence in rationalism and the repudiation of its artistic offspring, realism, were a marked shift of interest away from observed experience and towards the act of observation itself, and a sense of the absurdity of human existence. In the twentieth century, the Absurd has often been treated with great solemnity. But when Spanish writers come to explore and express modern man's bewilderment at the apparent futility and meaninglessness of his existence, their treatment, however tragic in its final implications, invariably includes an element of the grotesque comedy associated with the ordinary use of the word absurd. Comic irony is an essential part of the artistic vision of virtually all the writers to be considered in this chapter, and it clearly represents in most cases a serious assertion of the folly of taking life seriously. The peculiar attraction exercised by the theme of the circus, particularly its clowns, on writers and painters of this period, is a manifestation of the same outlook.

Given that life is wretched and absurd, the most pointless activity in which an artist can engage is that of copying it—a further reason for the devaluation of realist maxims. The move away from realism is the central theme of Ortega's famous essay of 1925, *La deshumanización del arte*. Although Ortega presents his views as an analysis of the very latest trends in the arts, with some predictions for the future, the essay in fact describes characteristics which can be discerned in the Spanish novel from the very first years of the century. Ortega's often extremely perceptive account of the state of the arts has sometimes been derided because of its failure as a prophetic document, but part of such criticism stems from the misleading nature of the term *deshumanización*. Ortega's real argument is simply that the nineteenth century's tendency to confuse life with art, and therefore to assign to the latter the function of representing reality, was an aberration from which artists in the twentieth century have happily recovered. Since he also makes it clear that he is not talking about popular entertainment, but about the kind of art that appeals only to an educated minority, his account of the direction in which art seemed to be moving in 1925 is illuminating and substantially correct. Indeed, the substance of his argument has long since become a commonplace of artistic history.

When applied to literature, the concept of *deshumanización* has sometimes been understood as describing a kind of writing which somehow bears no relation to the realities of human life. But as Ortega explains in his essay, and in *Ideas sobre la novela* (1925), and even in the much earlier *Meditaciones del Quijote* (1914), the dehumanisation in question means little more than the greatly reduced importance of narrative and description in literature. This, too, is fair comment on much of the prose fiction of the early part of the century. The painstaking accumulation of descriptive detail which the realists felt obliged to make tends to be replaced in modern novels by a series of rapid impressions. Historically, a pendulum effect is clearly visible. Just as some Spanish poetry in the latter part of the nineteenth century had seemed ashamed of being poetic, and had tried to disguise itself as rhymed novels, philosophy, sociology, or journalism, so the twentieth-century novel often leans towards techniques more commonly associated with poetry. Mallarmé's poetic aim of depicting not the thing but the effect it produces could well be regarded as that of the impressionistic techniques of several novelists at this time. Novels of the period also display an often ostentatious disregard for (and sometimes deliberate mockery of) the common reader's appetite for knowing 'what happened next', and his willingness to imagine the events in the narrative actually taking place. The use of myths and legends, the device of making literature out of already familiar literature, focuses attention on the treatment instead of the narrative, on how the story is told, not what it tells.

A further important characteristic of novels at this time is the pre-occupation with authorial perspective already referred to as typical of the general philosophical outlook of the age. This preoccupation naturally affected the novel more directly and obviously than other genres. Once again, Ortega's observations came rather late in the day. When he pursues his investigation of *perspectivismo* into the arts in his writings of the twenties, although he claims that he is delineating the 'theme of our time', he strangely makes no reference to contemporary Spanish prose fiction. Yet by the time he wrote *El tema de nuestro tiempo*, *La deshumanización del arte*, and *Sobre el punto de vista en las artes* (1924), novelists like Unamuno, Valle-Inclán, Pérez de Ayala, and Miró had already manifested their dissatisfaction with writing from the single, fixed perspective of even the most impersonal and omniscient conventional narrative viewpoint, and had tried, in different ways, to transcend the limitations of such a perspective.

The first Spanish novelist to make a radical break with conventional realist narrative was Miguel de Unamuno (1864-1936), though he did not do this until his second novel, *Amor y pedagogía*, of 1902. His first novel, *Paz en la guerra* (1897),[2] still remains broadly within the old conventions, and contains, as Unamuno observed in a preface to its second edition of 1923, 'pinturas de paisaje y dibujo y colorido de tiempo y lugar', all of which were to disappear from his fiction from 1902 onwards. *Amor y pedagogía* is at first sight an entirely improbable satiric fantasy about the downfall of a neo-Comtian, pseudo-Galtonian positivist, Avito Carrascal, whose half-baked ideas cause him to make a religion of science, and to try to breed and educate an immaculate genius on strictly scientific principles. It is not, however, an anti-scientific tract, but an illustration of the incompatible demands of rational eugenics and pedagogy and deep natural impulses such as sexual and maternal love and the fear of death. Essential to Unamuno's thesis is the fact that Avito's plans go wrong from the start. For example, having decided that the proper mother for a genius is a blonde, dolichocephalic type, he suddenly falls in love with the dark, brachycephalic Marina, a personification of both instinct and tradition—Unamuno calls her 'la Materia', whereas Avito is 'la Forma'. So although Avito struggles to bring up his son in strict observance of all the rites of the new religion, Marina constantly sabotages his efforts with outpourings of maternal affection, tainted with superstition and religious indoctrination of the other kind. Avito is acutely aware of his failures, the sins against his faith which he both permits and commits. 'Caíste, caíste, y volverés a caer', he murmurs to himself throughout the novel. So although when the genius is old enough to fall in love, and is spurned by his beloved, he promptly hangs himself, and although the novel *therefore* ends with the words 'El amor había vencido', we learn in an epilogue that Avito intends to repeat the experiment with his grandson, without repeating his previous falls from grace (though in Unamuno's next novel, *Niebla*, we meet him at prayer in a church, and learn that he has given up his old ideas).

Beneath the surface of this grotesque, and often amusing, farce, some of the preoccupations with which Unamuno was to wrestle in all his later writings are already apparent. The central ideas of *Del sentimiento trágico*, about truth and consolation, free will, immortality, are all raised in *Amor y pedagogía*, principally in Avito's discussions with the Unamuno-like Don Fulgencio Entrambosmares. As his name suggests, Entrambosmares is rather a shifty figure: philosophic mentor to both Avito and his son, author of the esoteric, unpublished *Ars magna combinatoria*, his deepest joy is his highly secret domestic life, and his passion for his elderly, golden-wigged wife. It is he who introduces the theme of 'erostratismo', urging Avito's son to have children as a means of achieving immortality, and it is he who first speaks of what the book calls the tyranny of logic. In the epilogue, Unamuno agrees with Fulgencio's sad observation that 'sólo la lógica da de comer', and adds: 'y sin comer no se puede vivir, y sin vivir no puede aspirarse a ser libre, *ergo* . . .'—therefore if we wish to be free we must be the slaves of logic. Two possible ways of breaking out of this paradox are considered, one of which accounts for the novel's unconventional manner. The epilogue goes on: 'Y siendo lo cómico una infracción a la lógica y la lógica nuestra tirana, la divinidad que nos esclaviza, ¿no es lo cómico un aleteo de libertad, un esfuerzo de emancipación del espíritu?' The other possibility derives from Unamuno's persistent idea, also expressed here by Fulgencio, that human life is like acting a role in a novel or a play. Unamuno finds the idea disturbing. In *Recuerdos de niñez y de mocedad*, which dates mainly from 1892, Unamuno had recalled with apprehension how as a child he used to tell stories to his schoolfriends at playtime, and kill off the characters when the bell for lessons sounded, regardless of whether or not they deserved to die. Fulgencio wonders if from time to time we may not be able to interpolate a *morcilla* or ad-lib into our part, which the Great Script-writer did not bargain for. One sort of *morcilla*, or 'metadramatic' moment when we rise above the script, thinks Fulgencio, might be to commit suicide—an idea which was to be treated more thoroughly in Unamuno's next novel. But these discussions end on a characteristic note of doubt. In the epilogue, Fulgencio wonders guiltily if he was responsible for the perhaps senseless suicide of Avito's son, while Unamuno wonders if he should have written two alternative endings to the novel, so as to force the reader into his own state of existential doubt.

Amor y pedagogía naturally perplexed a public accustomed to a different kind of prose fiction. The unconventional epilogue is followed by a treatise on making birds out of folded paper. As it happens, this was actually a lifelong hobby of the Rector of Sala-manca University, but the treatise is a burlesque both of comprehen-sive philosophical systems and modern artistic theories. Unamuno impudently justifies its inclusion by explaining that his publisher wants to include the book in a series of volumes of uniform thickness, and as it stands it is too thin. The reaction of some writers and critics to this kind of ironic levity was to complain that *Amor y pedagogía* was not a novel at all, to which Unamuno impatiently replied that if readers did not care to regard it as a *novela*, let it be called a *nivola*. In his 'prólogo-epílogo' to the second edition of *Amor y pedagogía*, he defines *nivolas* as 'relatos dramáticos acezantes, de realidades íntimas, entrañadas, sin bambalinas ni realismos en que suele faltar la verdadera, la eterna realidad, la realidad de la personalidad'. For the next twelve years, however, Unamuno wrote neither *novelas* nor *nivolas*. This was probably due less to any sense of discouragement than to his being too busy with other things. During this period, in addition to his academic duties as Professor of Greek and Rector of the University, he produced a huge number of articles and essays, the two books *Vida de don Quijote y Sancho* (1905) and *Del sentimiento trágico de la vida* (1913), a good deal of poetry, and most of the short stories eventually collected in *El espejo de la muerte* (1913). But in 1914 he published *Niebla*, this time subtitled 'nivola' so that there should be no mistake, and once again treating what for him were very serious matters in a disconcertingly comic manner. *Niebla* begins by asserting that existence precedes essence. This was no new idea to Unamuno in 1914. *Amor y pedagogía* already implies that man has no identity until he begins to commit himself to choice. In *Vida de don Quijote*, Unamuno pays approving attention to Cervantes's use of the old Spanish saying that man is the child of his works, and to the fact that Alonso Quijano, or whatever his name was, was nobody before he chose to become Don Quixote. Augusto Pérez of *Niebla* is a man who has improbably managed to reach marriageable age without having acquired any identity whatsoever. After a while, however, and as a result of a sequence of events so absurdly arbitrary that it would appear that Unamuno (a great admirer of *Don Álvaro, o la fuerza del sino*, it may be recalled) is alluding to the workings of some inscrutable destiny, Pérez acquires a provisional identity as the *novio* of Eugenia. But it is so provisional that when Eugenia disappears with her lover on the eve of the wedding, Augusto, who until recently had not even been aware of the problem of his authentic existence, now finds his lack of it so critical that he contemplates suicide. But first he takes what was for a fictional character in 1914 a very unusual step—though Calderón would not have been surprised by it, and it has become less unusual again since 1914: he goes to Salamanca to ask the advice of the well-known writer Miguel de Unamuno. When Unamuno reveals that Augusto is only a fictional character, with no reality outside Unamuno's imagination, and who cannot therefore choose even to kill himself, Augusto retorts with Unamuno's own assertion (in *Vida de don Quijote*) that there is a sense in which characters create their authors, and that eventually Unamuno will exist only in and through the existence of his fictional creations. The reminder of his own death naturally upsets the author of *Del sentimiento trágico*, who thereupon resolves to kill Pérez, and in what remains of the novel, apparently does so.

The seriousness with which this fantastic fabrication further explores the existential problems raised in Unamuno's earlier books is beyond question. Augusto's serenity while he still thinks he can die as an act of conscious and independent choice turns into stark terror when it seems that in fact his death will be the result of an indifferent creator's whim (Unamuno wipes a single, furtive tear from his eye after condemning him to death). The great teleological importance to us as human beings of the difference between the two ways of dying is acutely felt by Unamuno; but the fact is that he does not know, does not even venture to guess, the answer. The mood of doubt is maintained beyond the text of the novel, in the famous pair of prologues. Augusto's friend, Víctor Goti, claims that Augusto did in fact commit suicide, and that Unamuno's version of his death in the novel is a lie; Unamuno's prologue naturally denies this accusation.

As a character in *Niebla*, Unamuno assumes the role of a god against whom, if he exists, it is the duty of human beings to struggle and rebel. Perhaps the rebellion will achieve nothing in the way of changing our fate; but that is not its point. It will restore a certain dignity to human existence on the only possible terms acceptable to a genuinely existential outlook. *Niebla* reiterates the existential ethic which Unamuno elaborated in *Del sentimiento trágico*, for which, as he acknowledged, he was indebted to Senancour's *Obermann*: we must live *as if* what we need to believe were true, for by so doing we shall at least make arbitrary annihilation of the kind that occurs in 'Unamuno's version' of Augusto's death a monstrous injustice. The 'as-if' postulate rests on even less than a faint hope, merely on doubt. But that is all Unamuno can offer. Not only in the two prologues, but throughout the novel, this doubt is expressed in a stubborn dialectic between Víctor Goti and Unamuno in his capacity as God. It is Goti, himself a novelist, who provides Augusto with one of the arguments he uses against Unamuno at Salamanca, namely that even fictional characters, once they have begun to act and therefore to acquire an identity, are governed by an inner logic with which their creator is powerless to interfere. It is also Goti who expresses the real Unamuno's view of the creative nature of doubt: 'Y es la duda lo que de la fe y del conocimiento, que son algo estático, quieto, muerto, hace pensamiento, que es dinámico, inquieto, vivo'.

After *Niebla*, Unamuno's fiction turns its attention more completely to the question of what constitutes authentic existence and personal identity. In the three stories published between 1916 and 1920 and collected in *Tres novelas ejemplares y un prólogo* (1910), a fairly simple theory of personality is expounded. To Oliver Wendell Holmes's division of human personality into three selves—the one we think we are, the one others think we are, and the one we 'really' are (as God would see us)—Unamuno adds a fourth: the self we desire to be, the 'querer ser'. This last he deems the most important existentially, since it is the one that determines behaviour, or at least that part of it which Unamuno regards as most important. In all three stories the circumstances are artificially arranged so that the 'querer ser' of the protagonists is realised in action. But it is to be presumed that this is only for the sake of dramatising Unamuno's point. If their will to be a certain kind of person had been frustrated by circumstances, there would have been no exemplary tale, but the will would have conditioned their identity in the same way. The willed selves of the three protagonists are manifestly not the same as their 'real' selves, but they all succeed, at least for a time, in fashioning a self-for-others in accordance with their 'querer ser'.

The years during which he wrote these stories were turbulent ones for Spain and for Unamuno. His vigorously anti-German attitudes during the European war brought him increased notoriety and the enmity of the political Right. 1917 was a very grim year for Spain, and Unamuno's publication in that year of *Abel Sánchez*, a harrowing story of a man devoured by hatred and envy, owes a good deal to national circumstances at the time it was written. The general strike, serious regionalist manifestations, the revelation that the newly formed *Juntas militares de defensa* meant to interfere directly in politics in order to protect the army's interests against those of the general public, provided a mass of evidence, if any were needed, in support of the view of writers like Machado, Ortega, and Salvador de Madariaga, that Cain-like envy is Spain's special national curse. Unamuno's 'historia de pasión' explicitly acknowledges the reflection of a national vice in its last pages, when Joaquín exclaims: '¿Por qué nací en tierra de odios? En tierra en que el precepto parece ser: "Odia a tu prójimo como a tí mismo"'.

But allusions to national preoccupations form only a very small part of *Abel Sánchez*. The novel (which Unamuno called a *novela,* not a *nivola,* now) is a good deal more 'like life' than Unamuno's previous fiction. At one level it is indeed a serious psychological study of a singular but not entirely unrealistic paranoid personality. But beyond that it is yet another investigation of the enigma of authentic existence. By taking the story of Cain and Abel as the basis of his novel, Unamuno chooses a tragic passion that is ideal for his purposes: the essence of this kind of envy, he argues, is that we feel it for someone we think inferior to ourselves, but who is more highly esteemed by others. Moreover, the grounds for esteem, in the novel, are as baffling as those of the divine injustice of the story told in Genesis. Although Joaquín Monegro, unlike Augusto Pérez, has a sort of identity at the start of the novel, it has always been inexplicably eclipsed by the personality of his childhood companion Abel, and Joaquín's courtship of Helena is undertaken in a spirit of affirming his independent identity. When Helena marries Abel instead, Joaquín describes his own experience as a rebirth, but into hell. Thereafter his authentic existence is totally defined by his hatred of Abel. This may be why the novel is entitled *Abel Sánchez* when in fact it is the story of Joaquín Monegro. But in the tortured self-interrogation of his 'Confesión', Joaquín also wonders *why* his whole existence has come to mean only the existence of his hatred. He makes repeated attempts to cure himself—choosing a different identity—and repeatedly he fails. The novel's theory of identity is therefore very different from that of the *Tres novelas ejemplares*. Not only is Joaquín's 'querer ser' existentially ineffective, but the other three identities of the 'prólogo' are replaced by quite a different duality. On the one hand, Joaquín's identity is defined as the history of his deeds and sentiments; but his failures to escape from a hateful personality imply some sort of fatally predetermined essence. He even wonders if his hatred may not have preceded his birth and may not survive his death in some way. Unlike most later existentialists who also recognise the force of the argument which says that man has no given essence, Unamuno cannot rid himself entirely of the notion that an extra-human perspective might reveal (as Miguel de Unamuno revealed to Augusto Pérez) that we are pawns in a game whose rules we cannot know. And even when Unamuno tries to resign himself to the idea that man is no more than the history of his deeds, he notes, always sadly, that with each act of choice we leave behind a series of what he neatly called 'ex-future selves'.

To the end of his life Unamuno continued to probe into the complexities of essence and existence, and of different modes of existence, mainly in short works like *Tulio Montalbán y Julio Macedo* (1920), and plays like *Sombras de sueño* (1926), *El otro* (1926), and *El hermano Juan o el mundo es teatro* (1934). By the time he wrote these works, Unamuno was a very famous figure both in Spain and abroad, and there is no doubt that they reflect a keen personal awareness of the division of personality into a public and a private self. Although Unamuno was emphatically never a man to shun publicity or to miss an opportunity for self-dramatisation, it is nevertheless clear from his writings that the great weight of his 'legend'—as he was accustomed to call a man's existence-for-others—was often a matter which preoccupied him deeply. During his exile, Unamuno explored one aspect of the subject in *Cómo se hace una novela* (1927). The book is partly a series of personal reflections on his exile, but through them is threaded the story of a character called U. Jugo de la Raza, who one day finds a novel on a bookstall which tells him that when he gets to the end of it he will die. Again Unamuno is exploiting the idea that existence is like a novel written by its protagonist, and again the story postulates the possibility that we are also more than our novel. Jugo had no novel until he chanced on one in the bookstall. Without his novel he would, of course, have no authentic existence; yet if he had no novel to come to the end of, perhaps he would not die. In other words, if we are more than the history of our deeds, perhaps part of us will survive the ending of the history. Unamuno's last treatment of this major theme of his life's work was *La novela de don Sandalio, jugador de ajedrez* (1930), a brief master-piece of quite remarkable subtlety and complexity, which in addition to its challenging and ingenious thesis (too intricate to be summarised in a few words), reveals perhaps better than any of Unamuno's works his very considerable skill in guiding the reader towards understand-ing by means of an extremely careful use of imagery and symbolism.

Two of Unamuno's later works are sometimes taken to show that his fiction became more 'human' in his old age—though such an assessment must take an odd view of the profoundly human problems raised by a novel like *Niebla*. They are *La tía Tula* (1921) and the short novel *San Manuel Bueno, mártir* (1931). *La tía Tula*, like *Abel Sánchez*, has a basically realistic narrative framework, though it still lacks the descriptive 'bambalinas' of conventional realism, and is pre-faced by an important retrospective analysis of the novel, called, with characteristic twentieth-century irony, 'Prólogo que puede saltar el lector de novelas'. Part of the novel's purpose is to study the psychology of a woman with intensely powerful maternal impulses and a fierce loathing of the impurity of physical sexuality. But the book, which was conceived and partly written in 1902, the year of *Amor y pedagogía*, is also about the possibility of establishing, through education, a quasi-religious tradition in a family setting which will to some extent achieve the self-perpetuation of its founder. The signifi-cance of Tula's successful attempt to found such a cloistered com-munity is enhanced by the use of the thematic metaphor of the beehive, whose existential implications hardly need pointing out: there is no such thing as a queen egg in the hive, the identity of bees does not depend on physical maternity, but on the ministrations of worker bees, the sterile females, or 'tías', who thus pass on more of themselves than the fertile mother.

However, as any reader of *Del sentimiento trágico* will appreciate, Tula's attempt at surviving death is only a substitute for the real thing: personal immortality guaranteed by God. To this central pre-occupation Unamuno returned in *San Manuel Bueno*, only a few years before his own death. As in *Del sentimiento*, we are shown the absolute incompatibility of consolation and truth. The priest Don Manuel, who does not believe in an after-life, conceives it his duty to preach the comforting lie, for the sake of his flock, right up to the fearful moment of his own death. This, as it happens, was the message of an essay called *La vida es sueño* which Unamuno had written thirty-three years earlier: when a community has the good fortune to live cocooned in the comfort of a traditional, collective dream—symbolised in *San Manuel* by the drowned village in the still lake whose surface reflects heaven—it may be a crime to wake them with the truth. The truth here is of course that a river runs through the lake, one of Jorge Manrique's rivers, 'que van a dar a la mar, que es el morir'. In this moving story, it is possible to see, perhaps more clearly than in any other work by Unamuno, his longing to be a very different person from the tormented, belligerent, ideological iconoclast known to the general public.[3]

It was not to be his fate to live out his last years in peace, however. The legend summoned him to further struggles. Elected to the parliament of the Republic, he grew increasingly disillusioned with what he saw as the disintegration of his vision of a new Spain. Franco's rebellion caught him in Salamanca, in the Nationalist zone, where for a while he lent his support to what he thought was a fight to save civilisation from left-wing barbarism. But he lived just long enough to realise his error, and to admit it nobly in one last, legendary affirmation of his personality, his famous and courageous public reply to the ravings of a Fascist general in Salamanca University in the autumn of 1936. Once more he was dismissed from his post and placed under house arrest. In this honourable state, which in many respects underlines all that was best in Unamuno, he died, on the last day of 1936. His reputation as a great man and a major writer is already secure, and though it is still early to say on which of his writings his renown will ultimately rest, the likelihood is that it will be his prose fiction. Although some critics still accuse him of a host of sins which boil down to the single deadly one of having neglected to represent everyday reality, it was Unamuno more than any other writer who brought the Spanish novel into the twentieth century, and who strove to turn it into an instrument of deep reflection on the human condition. Furthermore it was Unamuno who, when Sartre was in his cradle, and after his restless erudition had caused him to learn Danish in order to read Kierkegaard, wrote the first novels which can be called existentialist. Whether or not one shares their agony and perplexity, there is no longer any denying that his novels represent an important contribution to twentieth-century European literature. The old, foolish, indictment that they are carelessly written and incoherently constructed has been demolished by new generations of readers who possess the wit, and have taken the trouble, to observe the subtle skills of Unamuno's literary art.

Unamuno's near-contemporary, Ramón del Valle-Inclán (1866-1936), who differed from him in most respects, resembles him in having written literature which announced that a new century had dawned, and that art had better things to do than tell stories about the surface reality of contemporary life. An extravagantly eccentric personality, Valle-Inclán distinguished himself by the particular eccentricity of being a conservative in his youth and a radical in his old age. His first important contributions to literature were the *Sonatas* (1902-05), the four exotic fantasies in exquisitely worked language which mark a change of climate in Spanish prose fiction as surely as did *Azul* and *Prosas profanas* in poetry. The *Sonatas*, in fact, represent one of the few irruptions of pure *modernismo* into Spanish prose literature, fleeing from prosaic reality into the consolation of a wonderworld of beautiful artifice whose values are almost entirely aesthetic. Nevertheless, the 'escapism' of which *modernista* writing is often accused, as if it were some childish game, derives from just the same anguished vision of the absurdity of existence and the same sense of the irreconcilability of consolation and truth which prompted Unamuno to write *Del sentimiento trágico de la vida*. Valle-Inclán makes the point explicitly in the early pages of *Sonata de invierno*:

¡Oh alada y riente mentira, cuándo será que los hombres se convenzan de la necesidad de tu triunfo! ¿Cuándo aprenderán que las almas donde sólo existe la luz de la verdad son almas tristes, torturadas, adustas, que hablan en el silencio con la muerte y tienden sobre la vida una capa de ceniza? ¡Salve, risueña mentira, pájaro de luz que cantas como la esperanza!

Critics who demand moral seriousness of art have judged the *Sonatas* harshly for their indifference to the moral problems of the workaday world and their lack of relevance to human existence. But *fin-de-siècle* decadence, in which the *Sonatas* are steeped, for all its world-weariness, is not so much a matter of neglecting ethical questions as of commenting, at least by implication, on conventional contemporary values, particularly on the materialism, hypocrisy, and vulgarity of the middle classes. Valle-Inclán's affirmation of insolently archaic aristocratic principles, and his endowment of the Marqués de Bradomín with sincere Catholic faith in order that the sins of pride, sacrilege, fornication, and necrophily should afford him a voluptuous sense of guilt and terror, are as much a sneer at prevailing bourgeois morality as was his later degradation of Spanish society to the stature of grotesque puppets. Furthermore, the common view that Bradomín's exploits are Valle-Inclán's own daydreams has to ignore the irony that permeates this inversion of conventional standards, and Bradomín's consistent self-mockery, his own reminders that he is behaving like a character from literary fiction—*Werther, Salammbô, Tirant lo Blanch,* etc.—and his cynical amusement at the outrageous spectacle of his own behaviour.

The fourth *Sonata* had found Bradomín playing at novels of chivalry during the last Carlist War. The double attraction exercised over Valle-Inclán by the picturesque residue of ancient feudal society which still existed in his native Galicia, and the violent death-throes of Carlism in the seventies, which he saw as the irresistibly romantic last stand of a colourful past against the drabness of modern life, provoked him to active support of the Carlist cause, and to the publication of several works expressing nostalgia for a vanished era of noble lords and loyal vassals and no middle classes. His trilogy of novels about the Carlist War, *Los cruzados de la causa, El resplandor de la hoguera,* and *Gerifaltes de antaño* (1908-09), and the *Comedias bárbaras,* three dramas about the Galician patriarch Don Juan Manuel Montenegro, *Águila de blasón* (1907), *Romance de lobos* (1908), and *Cara de plata* (1922), are products of this phase in his development, though it is to be noted that the last-named play is a very late product. But these Galician works are not a Pereda-like celebration of the glory, poetry, and joy that was to be found in Spain before liberal democracy arrived. Both the novels and the dramas speak of the decay of the old world. Juan Manuel is a barbaric feudal lord, arrogant, violent, and autocratic, but also, Valle-Inclán would have us believe, magnificent in his animal vigour, his courage and generosity, a true father to his people. Yet, although he has six sons, both he and his vassals know him to be the last of his race, for in his sons (with the exception of 'Cara de Plata', who is different from both his father and his brothers) nobility has died out, and they are merely greedy, treacherous animals. Moreover, when Valle-Inclán added *Cara de Plata* to the other two plays in 1922, although its action takes place before that of the others, he makes Juan Manuel himself more of a tyrant, much less beloved of his people.[4]

In the years immediately before the 1914-18 War, Valle-Inclán wrote mainly for the theatre, and his work of this period will be considered in a later chapter. The war years themselves were even more decisive for Valle-Inclán than for other Spanish writers. It was widely expected that the traditionalist Valle-Inclán would support the German cause. But in 1915 he took up an unequivocally anti-German position. The troubles of 1917 and the government's repressive reaction to them increased his concern with Spain's political and social situation. In an interview of 1920 (published in *El Sol*, 3 September 1920), he stated that 'El Arte es un juego . . . No debemos hacer Arte ahora, porque jugar en los tiempos que corren es inmoral, es una canallada. Hay que lograr primero una justicia social'. By this time he had also elaborated his theory of the *esperpento*, the extraordinary and original technique on which much of his greatness as a writer depends. His play *Luces de Bohemia*, which contains his first and most important statement of the theory, was first published in the periodical *España* between July and October of 1920. In its twelfth scene, Valle-Inclán's spokesman, Max Estrella, makes the famous affirmations that 'España es una deformación grotesca de la civilización europea', and that therefore, 'el sentido trágico de la vida española sólo puede darse con una estética sistemáticamente deformada', a deformation which Max likens to the reflection of classical heroes in the distorting concave mirrors of the amusement arcades in Madrid's Callejón del Gato. This distortion produces the *esperpento*.

Precise analysis of the theory of the *esperpento*, like precise definition of which of Valle-Inclán's works qualify for the title, is unprofitable. The theory, as will readily be seen, constitutes something of a paradox, in that it advocates a technique of deformation in order to capture a reality which is said to be deformed in the first place. Moreover, although it can be argued that a strict interpretation of the terms of the theory makes it describe only two or three of Valle-Inclán's works, it is obvious that the techniques suggested by the theory are not only present in all Valle-Inclán's writing from now on, but were foreshadowed in much of his earlier work. What the theory does not say, but what Valle-Inclán's practice makes clear, is that he thinks that our normal vision of reality is already distorted, or at any rate that we refuse to look steadily at people and things as they really are. A guilty sense of identification makes Spaniards, and perhaps human beings generally, alter the evidence of their eyes by making benevolent assumptions about what goes on beneath the surface of reality, by investing with dignity, substance, and coherence what is really brutish, hollow, and absurd. And of course the ennobling fictions pass into literature—this is where the classical heroes come in —and invite responses of admiration and compassion to the spectacle of human behaviour. So Valle-Inclán's techniques are all designed to return our unwilling gaze to the surface of things, and to block our ways of escape into exculpatory understanding. To explain away the idiocy of much human behaviour we need a sense of depth and spiritual complexity. Valle-Inclán's rejoinder is to turn people into animals, dolls, puppets, silhouettes, masks—thus eliminating the third dimension where fictions breed. As one critic has said of the characters of the *esperpento,* 'they *are* what they *seem to be,* or they *seem to be* what they *are*'.[5] It is an audacious method, for while it is utterly unlike life, it aims at giving a truer interpretation of what life is like than did the realist novels of 'Don Benito el Garbancero', as Valle-Inclán rudely called Galdós.

The theory of the *esperpento* also says that deformation must be systematic, subject to a 'matemática perfecta'. There are vague echoes of Cubism here, as there are elsewhere in Valle's work, but once again it would be a mistake to pay close attention to systematic or geo-metrical aspects of his practice. *Luces de Bohemia* itself displays a remarkably unsystematic mixture of moods and material. Its parody of Madrid's literary Bohemia owes a good deal to the popular burlesques of well-known dramas and operas which flourished in the early years of the century.[6] Also, like Pérez de Ayala's *Troteras y danzaderas,* which portrays the same world, most of its characters are based on real people. Yet the drama also expresses Valle-Inclán's wholly serious indignation at Spain's political situation, and in this connection there are two characters—the Catalan anarchist and the mother of the baby killed by a police bullet—who are not deformed at all, but appeal directly to our sense of outrage and pity. Nor are Max's wife and daughter subjected to any deforming technique. Max himself, whose story is based on the life and death of Valle-Inclán's friend Alejandro Sawa, finds his potentially tragic stature degraded in the course of the action to one of grotesque farce, but he is at least aware of his transformation into a character in an *esperpento*, and so stands outside the process of deformation in a way that other characters do not.

Between *Gerifaltes de antaño* (1909) and *Tirano Banderas* (1926), most of Valle-Inclán's works are in dramatic form. This has given rise to much discussion as to whether they should be considered as theatre or as dialogue novels. The discussion has its serious points, and some attention will be given to them in Chapter 3, but it was not a matter in which Valle-Inclán himself was much interested. In any case, the fundamental unity of his writing after he had elaborated the theory of the *esperpento* in 1920 is more important than the division into drama and novel. His work after this date may appear to be very varied. Some of it—*Divinas palabras* (1920) and most of the pieces eventually collected in *Retablo de la avaricia, la lujuria y la muerte* (1927)—is once again set in Galicia, though a bestial, macabre, witch-infested Galicia whose existence was only hinted at in *Sonata de otoño* and the *Comedias bárbaras*. Then, to his earlier *Farsa de la cabeza del dragón* (1914), he added, in 1920, two more verse farces, *Farsa y licencia de la Reina Castiza* and *Farsa italiana de la enamorada del Rey*, to form the trilogy pointedly entitled *Tablado de marionetas para educación de príncipes*. The three works to which he actually gave the subtitle of *esperpento*, collected in *Martes de Carnaval* (1930), are *Los cuernos de don Friolera* (1921), *Las galas del difunto* (1926), and *La hija del capitán* (1927). Finally there are his last great novels, *Tirano Banderas* (1926), and the first two and a half volumes of his projected cycle of nine novels under the general title of *El ruedo ibérico*—*La corte de los milagros* (1927), *Viva mi dueño* (1928), and the unfinished *Baza de espadas* which was first published in *El Sol* in 1932.

In spite of the diversity of subject-matter that is evident even in this brief catalogue of his post-war work, certain underlying characteristics are common to all of it, and may be tentatively summarised as follows. Firstly, it all derives from a bitterly critical vision of Spanish reality (rural, metropolitan, plebeian, aristocratic, contemporary, historical) which seeks to degrade it, either by brutal *tremendismo* (*Divinas palabras*, the *Retablo* pieces), or by cruel ridicule (*Don Friolera*, the farces), or by both (the novels). The vision involves a clear commitment to politico-social principles of a revolutionary kind. Usually this commitment means no more than a general condemnation of injustice and corruption, as in the account of the obscene barbarity and hypocrisy of the villagers in *Divinas palabras*, or in his portrayal of a fictional Latin American dictator in *Tirano Banderas*. It is unlikely that Valle-Inclán's fiction achieved anything in the way of making ideological converts, but at least he establishes that he regards as enemies of the public good such folk as kings, aristocrats, priests, army officers, the police, conservative politicians, and the bourgeoisie.

The distorting, degrading vision is achieved partly, as has been said, by depriving his characters of any dimension of depth, by likening them to animals, dolls, and puppets, catching them and often immobilising them in grotesque postures, refusing to acknowledge that they mean to say or do anything different from their actual words and behaviour. The tangle of identities which preoccupied Unamuno is thus swept away and replaced by the stark proposition that our whole identity is just what it appears to be for others. But there is another side to Valle's technique of deformation. In a famous interview with Martínez Sierra (published in *ABC* on 7 December 1928), he spoke of three possible perspectives from which an author may view his characters: the Homeric view of them as superhuman beings, the Shakespearian attitude that they are creatures of flesh and blood like the author, and the 'demiurgic' conception of them as 'seres inferiores al autor, con un punto de ironía'. Valle-Inclán usually chooses the last alternative. The force of these observations had already been brought out by *Los cuernos de don Friolera*, which offers three versions of the same story: the sad case of Friolera's marital honour, exacerbated by the fact that he is a military man, and, as all the world should know, 'en el Cuerpo de Carabineros no hay cabrones'. The third version is an Andalusian *romance de ciego*, and clearly represents a 'de rodillas' exaltation of a traditional Spanish 'classical hero', and as such provokes the disgust of Valle-Inclán's *alter ego*, Don Estrafalario. The main, middle version, although an undoubted *esperpento*, we must take to be the least unrealistic of the three, and it is therefore interesting to note that Friolera, absurd puppet as he is, has his moments of pitiful humanity when he commands compassion, and even recognises the absurdity of his situation. At such moments Valle-Inclán is clearly seeing him from an 'en pie' perspective, as in fact he sees a number of characters in his later works—Feliche Bonifaz of *El ruedo*, the Indian Zacarías of *Tirano Banderas*, Fermín Salvochea of *Baza de espadas*. But the first version, the coarse puppet-show of the Galician-Portuguese *bululú* Fidel, is the one that Don Estrafalario regards as the most authentic reflection of the reality of the events: 'Sólo pueden regenerarnos los muñecos del Compadre Fidel!'. The same message is imparted by *Las galas del difunto*, where we see Zorrilla's Don Juan Tenorio reflected in the concave mirrors of the Callejón del Gato. Until Spanish audiences appreciate that the only fitting way of presenting this traditional Spanish hero is as the grotesque protagonist of a lewd fairground farce, says Valle-Inclán, they will not apprehend the true 'sentido trágico de la vida española'.

The theories of perspective enunciated by Don Estrafalario also have something to say about the element of time. This was a matter that evidently concerned Valle-Inclán deeply, though it must be recognised that his conclusions remain somewhat obscure. Don Estrafalario ponders, in typical modern fashion, on the importance to all art of a sense of the imminence of death. 'Todo nuestro arte nace de saber que un día pasaremos'. When his friend Don Manolito thereupon accuses him of wishing to be like God, he replies, 'Yo quisiera ver este mundo con la perspectiva de la otra ribera'. This is an idea which is obviously linked with the Gnostic philosophy expounded in Valle-Inclán's strange statement of aesthetic theory in *La lámpara maravillosa* (1916). There is a good deal of occult mumbo-jumbo in this book, but most of it can fairly be interpreted as a metaphor of artistic perception, and in this respect the theories bore interesting fruit not only in the originality of the structure of his last novels,[7] but in a general concern to attain a perspective beyond that imposed by chronological time. Valle-Inclán was much absorbed by the idea that only by abstracting things from the flow of time can one capture their true significance. He was also inclined to believe in the old idea that there are moments in human lives, notably those preceding death, when everything seems to hold still, and, lit by a sudden ultra-telluric gleam, renders up its eternal meaning. Although there is no necessary connection between the two ideas, they have common roots in the theories of *La lámpara*. Among the book's 'ejercicios espirituales' or themes for meditation, there are such statements as: 'Cuando se rompen das normas del Tiempo, el instante más pequeño se rasga como un vientre preñado de eternidad', and 'Sólo buscando la suprema inmovilidad de las cosas puede leerse en ellas el enigma bello de su eternidad'. Such notions had had their effect on Valle-Inclán's art from the beginning of his career: a notable example is the freezing of persons and actions into a tableau, with its 'silencio de cosas inexorables', and 'fatalidad de un destino trágico' in the climactic final moments of *Sonata de primavera*. But their most important repercussions on his literary technique are in his habit of presenting his vision of reality in static, synthetic *cuadros*, rather than by means of an unfolding narrative. Although all Valle-Inclán's works do contain a linear, chronological sequence of events, the truth he wishes to impart does not emerge from the unfolding action, as is usual in fiction. The reader does not need to know any 'outcome' in order to apprehend the truth. The discovery, for instance, that Friolera finally shoots his baby daughter when aiming at his wife and her lover adds nothing to our understanding of his predicament. In a sense it may seem that the circular structure of the novels of the *Ruedo ibérico*[8] works against this technique, for it is certainly true that a full appreciation of the implications of Chapter 1 of either *La corte de los milagros* or *Viva mi dueño* depends not only on relating it to Chapter 9, but on having passed through the 'concentric circles' of the intervening pairs of chapters. But there is still no question of 'desenlace'. It is quite clear that the circular structure is essentially a further attempt to break out of what Valle-Inclán regarded as the mistake of trying to understand reality as a chronological sequence of events.

Finally, the most important element which gives unity to all Valle-Inclán's work is his astonishing use of language. Just as he contrived to break reality into fragments and remould them into remarkable works of art, quite unlike the original, but offering a highly suggestive interpretation of it and a powerful set of feelings about it, so Valle-Inclán drew on a multitude of linguistic resources and welded them into an inimitably personal instrument of expression. Some of what was once thought to be the result of a fantastic capacity for linguistic invention turns out in fact to have its roots in other writings —including his own, for Valle-Inclán was much given to reworking his own earlier material.[9] But since Julio Casares's malicious *mot* to the effect that in Valle's work, as in nature, nothing is ever wasted or destroyed, his enormous talent for transforming assimilated material into brilliantly original creations, far from diminishing his prestige, has generated increasing admiration. In his language, his major achievement is certainly what Antonio Risco's recent study (*La estética de Valle-Inclán*) calls 'nivelación de jerarquías', or, quoting Juan Ramón Jiménez, 'un habla total'. That is to say that his literary style fuses together a diversity of linguistic strains—poetic metaphor, Madrid gutter-slang, Americanisms, rustic Galician, high-society affectation, gypsy and criminal vernacular, his own ingenious neologisms—which in a lesser writer would jostle awkwardly together, into a linguistic instrument of quite extraordinary concision, force, and wit. *La lámpara maravillosa* bears witness to Valle-Inclán's serious concern with forging a literary style which he intended should redeem the language of his people from the insipid pseudo-traditionalism and academic pomposity into which it had fallen. The magnificently exuberant inventions of his last years, above all *Tirano Banderas* and *El ruedo ibérico*, offer the means of grace and the hope of glory in such a redemption. Like Unamuno's works, they are at last attracting attention as major contributions to modern European literature. Unlike Unamuno, however, and unfortunately for Valle-Inclán's deserved reputation as a writer of universal importance, his remarkable stylistic gifts, coupled with his preoccupation with 'el sentido trágico de la vida española', make most of his work virtually untranslatable. One need only reflect for a moment on the problems presented by the mere titles of his works—*Los cuernos de don Friolera, La corte de los milagros, Baza de espadas,* or even *El ruedo ibérico* itself—to appreciate how much of the explosively allusive quality of his language would have to be lost in the language of a different culture.

Pío Baroja (1872-1956)[10] is a most disconcerting phenomenon in the literary history of the period. Although he is obviously closely related to his major contemporaries by his philosophical outlook, his literary art is as different as can be imagined from the prevailing characteristics of early twentieth-century prose fiction, and contradicts most of the general statements made at the beginning of this chapter. Nevertheless (or perhaps because of this) his reputation is very great, especially in Spain, where of all his generation of outstanding writers, he is the one who is most admired and read today. His influence on the Spanish novel of the post-Civil War period has been incomparably greater than that of all his contemporaries put together. Non-Spanish readers of Baroja may find this puzzling, but it is an indisputable fact which should never be forgotten.

It may perhaps be misleading to start by describing Baroja's novels as his 'literary art'. This irascible, uncouth individualist who was opposed to almost everything—religion and the Church, all political systems, the State, Spain and Spaniards, Jews, Frenchmen, the list is endless—was also against Culture. His theories of creative fiction[11] can be reduced to three main assertions: that art is vastly inferior to life, and should therefore be based on observation of life; that style is ideally a matter of expressing oneself briefly, directly, and exactly; and that the novel is a shapeless, informal genre which should be judged on the strength of its capacity to entertain the reader. There is, of course, a certain amount of truculent exaggeration in these theories, provoked as much by Baroja's notorious lack of self-assurance as by his disapproval of aesthetic artifice such as Valle-Inclán's, by Ortega's anti-realistic theories of art, and by early criticism of his own works as 'badly written'. Baroja even suggested that having abandoned the medical profession and having failed to make a success out of running a bakery, there was nothing left for him to do but take up writing novels. The element of pose in such attitudes is evident in the very quantity of Baroja's published thoughts on how one should write prose fiction, and also in statements of a rather different kind, such as: 'escriber con sencillez es muy difícil y exige mucho tiempo'. But the resolve not to distinguish between literature as art and literature as entertainment was sincere enough, and Baroja's lifelong, unashamed fondness for adventure yarns of a popular kind is an important factor in his formation as a writer.

But what in the end is most disconcerting about Baroja is not his unadorned style nor his unfashionable determination to appeal to a wide public, but his extraordinary disregard of all the traditional decencies of the novelist's art. One cannot help wondering to what extent the high esteem in which he is held is really due to his attitude to life, rather than to his way of writing. His steady, honest, pessimistic vision of the world, with its deep sense of compassion and urge to moral justice, is a noble and serious one. Accusations that the philosophical content of his novels is shallow and naïve are unjust. Baroja, who read widely and pondered deeply on what he had read, possessed a gift for expressing a perfectly serious philosophical vision of modern life with great simplicity and clarity. There is nothing naïve or superficial about the intellectual substance of novels like *El árbol de la ciencia* or *La sensualidad pervertida*; it is only that Baroja's habit of plain speaking makes their ideology easy to understand, which is not always the sign of profundity or significance. Unlike Valle-Inclán, Baroja has certainly converted many a reader to his point of view. Gregorio Marañón has borne eloquent witness to the impact made on him and others like him by reading Baroja's bitter trilogy, *La lucha por la vida* (1904-05), as a young man.[12] Marañón called the novels three breaches in the wall of egotistical blindness which the Spanish bourgeoisie had built round itself so as to ignore the misery of the majority of Spaniards at the beginning of the century, and he attributes to Baroja a major role in creating a social conscience in middle-class youth at the time.

These are very solid virtues, and if Marañón is right, Baroja deserves his esteem as a writer of the first importance. But they are not qualities which in themselves make for great literary art. From a purely literary standpoint, and putting the matter as neutrally as possible, the reader of a typical Barojan novel has to abandon many of the principles by which he is accustomed to judge the excellence of prose fiction. The most important habit that has to be unlearnt is that of supposing that close reading of a novel, paying careful attention to the way things are said, will give a better understanding of its meaning and purpose than will a rapid and superficial perusal. The common idea that in a serious novel the characters and events are bound to signify something beyond their immediate relevance to the continuation of the narrative, and the common novelistic practice of using symbolic or allusive imagery in order to give body and feeling to the author's vision, are best forgotten when reading Baroja. Where such features exist, they seem to have crept in by accident, unknown to the author.

Their absence means that the questions one usually asks about the significance of any particular component and its relation to the total structure of the work will normally be irrelevant. In this sense Baroja's novels are indeed sacks into which he throws all sorts of oddments whose function is simply that they help fill the sack. It is a waste of time to seek connections between such oddments and an overall pattern, for none is intended. The rapid succession of unconnected events and anecdotes in a novel like *Zalacaín al aventurero* (1909) might conceivably reflect a Bergsonian attempt to extract from chronological time 'that real, concrete duration in which the past remains bound up with the present',[13] but we may be sure that it has little to do with Baroja's intentions when he wrote the novel. The two parts of *César o nada*, for example, have a very satisfying balance. César's idle existence in Rome, with its endless conversations and reflections on the cultural and religious heritage of the Eternal City, provides an apt and illuminating prelude to his whirlwind activity in the savage world of Castro Duro, where he is destroyed by the forces of tradition and religion, and as an ultimate irony ends his days as an apolitical aesthete, famous for his collection of the kind of artistic antiquities he had been so contemptuous of in Rome. But it seems that this is not how Baroja saw the novel. The first part is set in Rome because Baroja had been to Rome the year before, and had a store of observations about his visits to monuments and museums and the folk he had met in hotels, of which he wished to make use in a novel. Moreover, in later editions of the novel, Baroja inexplicably cut out the apparently barbed final allusion to the total collapse of César's former ideals—explicitly described as his reduction to 'nada'. In later editions we do not even know if he died from his gunshot wounds, and thus as a victim of his principles, or found some kind of middle course, in provincial Castile, between being Caesar and being nothing.

It is sometimes claimed that Baroja's monolinear, episodic narratives represent a bold attempt at a more radical kind of realism than had hitherto been conceived of. Baroja himself was well aware that the realist novels of the nineteenth century often did not so much copy life as rearrange its elements into meaningful interpretive patterns. He also held the odd but interesting view that there is an inherent conflict between the aim of giving a novel a coherent structure and that of presenting characters who are true to life, so that the novelist must choose between having a book with 'un aire desordenado', or characters with 'un aire falso'.[14] For Baroja, the great novels are the disorderly ones. He mentions, among others, *Don Quixote*, *Robinson Crusoe*, *Rob Roy*, *The Brothers Karamazov*, *David Copperfield*, and *War and Peace*—all basically episodic novels, their structure determined by the single fact of the protagonist's presence, as in the picaresque novel, and, of course, as in Baroja's own novels. If one thinks of novels like those of Unamuno, or of the cruder type of thesis novel, one can see what he is getting at, but as a theory of the art of fiction it is very debatable: there are plenty of novels which combine extremely life-like characters with both a strong conceptual structure and what Baroja calls, with mild disapproval, 'argumento cerrado y definitivo'. His remarks do, however, make it clear that the typical inconsequentiality of his own novels is intended to convey the impression which life actually gives us most of the time—a random succession of disjointed, insignificant happenings—and that Baroja can therefore be credited with a conscious desire to dispense with what for thirty centuries has been regarded as one of the principal functions of art: that of organising experience into meaningful patterns. The irrelevance, to anything, of some incidents in Baroja's books can be positively disturbing. When one reads, for example, in Chapter 3 of *Aventuras, inventos y mixtificaciones de Silvestre Paradox* (1901), that among the figures who populated the world of Silvestre's boyhood there was a woman called La Chaleca, '. . . mujer estrafalaria, vestida de una manera chocante, que a veces tenía la ocurrencia de ponerse una almohada sobre el vientre debajo de la falda para hacer creer que estaba embarazada', it is hard to suppress the impulse to wonder what she is doing in the novel, or at the very least, why she does this strange thing. But the words quoted constitute Baroja's total and only reference to La Chaleca.

As far as his way of writing is concerned, Baroja's much-quoted assertion of the ideal of action for action's sake takes on a rather special meaning. Although many of his novels express a coherent attitude to life, it is invariably to be found in what the characters say, not in what they do. Even the curious satirical allegory *Paradox, Rey* (1906), where for once the story is intended to 'signify' something, is nearly all in dialogue form. In many of his best-known novels the characters do little except talk, and the action of books like *La ciudad de la niebla* (1909), *El árbol de la ciencia* (1911), *El mundo es ansí* (1912), or *El gran torbellino del mundo* (1926) is often of only marginal relevance to the ideas expressed in the conversations which form the real substance of the novels. But Baroja also wrote books which are almost all action. His sea stories, such as *Las inquietudes de Shanti Andía* (1911), *El laberinto de las sirenas* (1923), *Los pilotos de altura* (1929), *La estrella del capitán Chimista* (1930), have been likened to Conrad's but they are much more likely to remind the English reader of Stevenson or Captain Marryat. (All three authors were read and admired by Baroja.) Here action really is for action's sake. Shanti Andía's 'inquietudes' are rarely allowed to interrupt the remarkable agglomeration of seafaring yarns, many of them quite fantastic, about buried treasure, slave-trading, mutiny, and other high adventure in the last days of sail. Action for action's sake is also the subject of the series *Memorias de un hombre de acción*.[15] Since the action in question stretches from the War of Independence to the middle of the nineteenth century, the series inevitably invites comparison with Galdós's *Episodios nacionales*, but the two projects have very different motives. Galdós's intention was to construct an interpretation of the past which would help explain the present; he therefore chose his subject-matter for its historical importance, though he then turned the history into novels by viewing it through the personal experience of a series of fictional characters. Baroja inverts these terms: though his protagonist is a basically historical one, Aviraneta's *Memorias* are merely a string of personal adventures, and offer no large or sustained insight into either the history of the period or the personality of the hero.

It must be admitted that Baroja's action-narrative is of lamentably poor quality, lacking the minimum of psychological depth needed to explain what motivates the characters (in spite of Baroja's wish that they should be life-like), and in the end extremely monotonous. The only excuse that can be made for these adventure yarns is that among the odds and ends Baroja has thrown into his sacks there are a number of fine things. Baroja's virtue is not that he wrote great novels, not even two or three, but that his novels invariably contain certain admirable features. In addition to the solid virtues already referred to, and in addition to his sincerity and intellectual honesty, he is a real master of two aspects of the novelist's art: conversation and description. The best conversations in his work are marvellously absorbing and convincing. Although they are typically contrived to tell the reader about the protagonist's attitude to life, and so take the form of an argument with someone who disagrees with him, the interlocutor is never a Socratic feeder, but defends a different point of view with sufficient vigour and conviction to give the reader, and sometimes the protagonist, honest cause to wonder who is right. The talking is also realistic in the sense that it is as far removed as can be imagined from the elegant domestic symposia of a Jane Austen or a Valera. Baroja's characters hesitate, contradict themselves, grow angry or impatient, find themselves at a loss for words and escape into frivolity or abuse, in a way that is normal in life but quite unusual in literature.

But what stays longest in the mind after reading one of Baroja's novels is a sensation of place, of physical atmosphere. His descriptive powers are hard to analyse, but it is here that one best appreciates the force of his remark about the difficulty of writing simply, for it is not just a matter of naming everything exactly, or of writing in a 'flat', or 'grey', or unadorned way, as some would have it. Images and metaphors are rare, it is true, but the components of each setting described are chosen with great care and skill, and are usually embellished with a considerable wealth of epithet. Although Baroja can, if he wishes, convey a vivid impression of a picturesque, sunlit, old Castilian town like Castro Duro, he is at his best in descriptions of big modern cities. No reader of *La lucha por la vida* is likely to forget the way in which, without any kind of falsification, Baroja contrives to convey the sad squalor and ugliness of the poor parts of Madrid in terms of a deeply moving aesthetic experience which also imparts, in spite of everything, a sense of vitality which sometimes comes close to actual optimism.

Such descriptions naturally find their way into the increasingly and perplexingly fashionable anthologies of Spanish literature. In a sense this is not unfitting, for (apart from their convenient brevity) they are still essentially oddments in the sack, and as such make more sense in an anthology than, say, a chunk torn out of one of Unamuno's novels. But on the other hand, Baroja's skill in evoking a physical atmosphere is what gives many of his novels their real strength and character. In *La ciudad de la niebla,* for instance, what sticks in the imagination and distinguishes Baroja as a writer is not the account of the escapades of a seedy group of revolutionaries, nor even the observations on life of María and her friends in Slough and Soho, but the feeling of being in the London, and even the Slough, of the period. This is Baroja's enduring merit as a literary artist. It was an unusual merit in the age of Unamuno and Valle-Inclán, but that is of course no reason why all three of them should not deserve a major place in literary history.

Unlike Baroja, who remained faithful to the outlook and literary manner he developed as a young member of the Generation of 1898, and whose novels therefore changed very little during the fifty years of his writing career, Ramón Pérez de Ayala (1880-1962) was always a restless literary experimenter. After he had completed his important contribution to the Generation's characteristic fiction in the early years of the century,[16] his experiments take the typical twentieth-century form of querying the artistic validity of traditional realism, emphasising the difference between art and life by drawing the reader's attention away from description and anecdote and towards artistic treatment, and inquiring into problems of perspective. His youthful rebelliousness persisted in his work for many years. His novels have been accused of being over-intellectual, nihilistic, and pornographic; and indeed the reader is often conscious of the triple legacy of his Jesuit education: a broad and solid culture, which often shows itself in a delight in pedantry for its own sake; an absence of any religious belief; and a somewhat morbid preoccupation with sordid aspects of sexual behaviour.

His first fictional experiment after *Troteras y danzaderas* (1913) was the trilogy *Prometeo, Luz de domingo,* and *La caída de los Limones* (1916), which Pérez de Ayala regarded as transitional between his earlier and later manners. The trilogy's subtitle, 'Novelas poemáticas de la vida española', indicates why. Like his four previous novels, part of their purpose is to convey a very unpleasant vision of Spain, a land of frustrated hopes, savage brutality, hateful malice, public corruption, stagnation, and degeneration. All three stories portray a particular national sickness which Alberto de Guzmán had described to Teófilo Pajares after the performance of the latter's play in *Troteras.* Spaniards, he said, hunger for the ideal and the infinite, aspiring to become like God. In the process of failing to achieve this ideal, they also fail even to become men. The stories of Marco Setiñano and his son, of Cástor Cagigal and of Arias Limón, make three human tragedies out of the theory, and insist on the national character of the dilemma.

Stylistically, however, the stories depart from the technique of *Troteras,* which was fundamentally realistic and drawn from life in spite of the often erudite allusions to other literature in the chapter titles. In the *novelas poemáticas* such allusions determine the structure of the stories, notably in *Prometeo,* which is less the story of Prometheus than that of the Odyssey. The function of this use of older literature is of course principally to reduce the importance of what happens in the narrative and call attention to what the author makes of the story in the new version. At the beginning of *Prometeo* Pérez de Ayala says bluntly that the reader already knows the story he is going to tell. Transposing Homer into a modern Spanish setting is in part, it must be recognised, simply the kind of intellectual game Pérez de Ayala enjoyed playing for its own sake, or so that the reader might have the small satisfaction of spotting that the modern Tiresias is (presumably) Unamuno, and so on. But it also has the more serious purpose of expressing comment on modern life by its constant degradation of the original model, thus anticipating Valle-Inclán's deformation of classical heroes in the *esperpento.* That is to say that as well as the homely fun of giving the new Nausicaa the name of Perpetua Meana, the Prometheus of the end of the story is even more of a tragic monster than the 'new Prometheus' of Mary Shelley and the Romantics. Similarly, in *Luz de domingo,* the modern version of the story of the daughters of the Cid becomes a sordid tragedy in which there is no longer any hope of just reprisals against the violators, while in *La caída de los Limones*, the heroic spirit of the *conquistadores*, whose blood runs in the veins of the Limón family, expresses itself, in modern times, in a demented act of rape and bestial murder.

The stories are 'novelas poemáticas' firstly because each short chapter is prefaced by a verse passage which anticipates, summarises, and comments on the following prose section. Pérez de Ayala's own justification of this experiment (also employed in the short stories collected in *El ombligo del mundo*; 1924) is interesting, but it does not go very far. The poems, he says, aspire to convey truth 'por un procedimiento más directo y sintético que analítico'.[17] Elsewhere he observed that 'muchas y enfadosas descripciones naturalistas ganarían en *precisión y expresividad* si se las cristalizase en un conciso poema, inicial del capítulo'.[18] So, like a Greek Chorus, they further reduce the anecdotal interest by saying, as it were: 'this is what is going to happen; now watch how it happens'. But more importantly, the mixture of verse and prose realises an idea which is absolutely central to all Pérez de Ayala's work up to 1921, and which was to be the actual subject of his next novel: the dual perspectives of spectator and actor, from which we may view human drama, our own or that of others. Throughout his writing there are characters who change, often suddenly, from one perspective to the other. A striking example is Alberto's sudden transformation from actor to spectator at the end of his affair with Meg in *La pata de la raposa*; after it, 'Alberto consideraba la vida como una obra da arte, como un proceso del hacer reflexivo sobre los materiales del sentir sincero, imparcial'. *Troteras y danzaderas* amplifies the idea, and the force of 'imparcial', in Alberto's observations on Verónica's reactions to *Othello*. Verónica has the gift of identifying with each character in turn, living out their dramas from the inside as though they were her own. Her lack of the spectator-artist's vision makes her reactions somewhat chaotic, but Alberto admires them all the same.

Spectator and actor therefore become two modes of understanding life, each deficient on its own. Alberto further identifies them with what he regards as the two highest human virtues. The objective perspective of the spectator engenders a sense of justice (so that we know that Othello is wronged and Iago is evil), and the subjective, 'lyrical' capacity for entering into the drama produces tolerance (so that Verónica is deeply and sympathetically aware of what prompts Iago's evil). The poems of the *novelas poemáticas* clearly adopt the spectator's perspective, and often an objective, harmonious, synthetic vision of events. Then the prose sections act out the drama in a narrative of human emotion and experience, so that we see and feel what the events mean to the individuals concerned.

Pérez de Ayala's next novel, *Belarmino y Apolonio* (1921), is his most ambitious experiment in the exploration of dual perspective. It has hardly any action in the normal sense of the term. At the heart of the book is a little novelette about the elopement and return of Pedrito and Augustias, but this is merely a sort of case history, to give the theories something to work on. The novel packs a great deal of varied material into its short length, not always harmoniously. Pérez de Ayala is never reluctant to turn aside from his main concerns to play with an idea that amuses him—the importance of puberty and the menopause to mystical experience, the idea that people sleep at different speeds—though some of these apparent digressions, like Guillén's long disquisition on the Breviary and the early history of the Church, have an important and at times subtle bearing on other parts of the novel. And the second chapter, which Pérez de Ayala, like Unamuno, sardonically recommends the 'lector impaciente de acontecimientos' to skip, contains the essence of the theory of 'visión diafenomenal' on which the whole novel is based. The chapter ends with the characteristically twentieth-century suggestion that now that the artist Lirio has made such a handsome sketch of the ugly street, the street itself should be knocked down.

The complex of perspectives which make up the structure of *Belarmino y Apolonio* is exceedingly intricate, and it is worth noting that the experiments with perspective extend far beyond the duality of outlook represented by the two shoemakers. In accordance with the theories of Lirio and Lario, the same events are often narrated from different points of view and moments in time. We are reminded at the start by Don Amaranto de Fraile of the ancient division of methods of philosophical inquiry into Aristotelian-relativist-scientific and Platonic-absolutist-religious—a division highly relevant to Belarmino's subsequent philosophical collapse. Characters are known by different names to different people. Different narrative styles are freely, not purposefully, mixed. And although the differences can invariably be defined as dichotomies, the total vision of the novel is multiphenomenal rather than diphenomenal. But at the centre of it all is the same basic matter of spectator and actor, personified in the grotesque exaggerations of the two cobblers who will not stick to their lasts. The theory of *Troteras* and the practice of *Prometeo* now become much more complicated, for although it is still Pérez de Ayala's view that the polarity of perspectives is a complementary one, and that the world can only be properly understood by combining them, the novel re-examines the question of which perspective—that of the philosopher Belarmino or that of the dramatist Apolonio—is really the spectator's and which the actor's. Even this question is treated in dualistic terms, for the prologue and epilogue of the novel adopt contradictory attitudes to the very attitudes represented by the incompatible cobblers. It would appear at first, as Don Amaranto pointed out, that we can identify Belarmino's philosophical vision with the detached, total vision of a spectator, and Apolonio's instinctive histrionics with the involvement of an actor intent only on interpreting his own role. But it is also true, as El Estudiantón argues, that Belarmino's would-be impartial contemplation of the way the world works is destroyed by his deep emotional response to the little tragedy of his adopted daughter, after which he lapses into *ataraxia* and stops philosophising. On the other hand, Apolonio, who speaks in verse, writes dramas, and reacts to every situation by immediately selecting the appropriate role in which to act it out, is a hollow man, always, says El Estudiantón, the spectator of his own drama. So El Estudiantón claims that the relation between their polarised perspectives is the opposite of what Don Amaranto supposed it to be. Don Amaranto continues to disagree. And there Pérez de Ayala leaves his cobblers and their commentators. Both points of view are tenable. That is what perspectivism means.

Belarmino y Apolonio attracted little interest in its day, even among the select minority of readers who might have been expected to welcome it as an interesting experiment in modern fiction. Whether because of this or because he felt he had exhausted the spectator/actor theme, Pérez de Ayala's next novel, published in two parts, *Luna de miel, luna de hiel* and *Los trabajos de Urbano y Simona* (1923), abandons the subject—though several of the characters continue to experience different kinds of *desdoblamiento*—and exploits instead what had been only subsidiary features in Pérez de Ayala's earlier work. The important conceptual elements of *Belarmino y Apolonio* had tended to obscure the fact that Pérez de Ayala handles language with great authority and is master of a wide variety of styles, from a delicate tone of lyrical fantasy to a brutal realism which causes shock and revulsion. There is often an element of pastiche in his style. Some of the juvenilia collected in *Bajo el signo de Artemisa* (1924) read like a precocious schoolboy's literary exercises 'after the manner of' some other writer, which is perhaps what they were. Even in his mature writing it is his habit to adopt a certain manner for a few paragraphs, and then drop it in favour of another. His mock-pedantic style can be somewhat laboured, as in the scene in *La caída de los Limones* when Arias kicks the dog Delfín through the air into Dominica's lap. Much more acceptable is the device in *Belarmino y Apolonio* of presenting Felicita's fears about Novillo's death in the manner of an ancient legend or fairytale, for both characters are unrealistic caricatures anyway. But whereas in *Belarmino* the different styles do not always blend happily, and so give an impression of an ingenious patchwork of different kinds of literary virtuosity, in *Luna de miel* and its sequel, Pérez de Ayala has succeeded in forging something like his own version of Valle-Inclán's 'habla total'—though the emphasis, in spite of bits of Asturian dialect and blunt descriptions of peasant life, is always on elegant artifice and linguistic ornament.

Like *Belarmino y Apolonio, Luna de miel* and *Los trabajos* attempt various things. The story, if it can be so called, is about the education of children, so, as we should expect, there are allusions to Plato, Calderón (*La vida es sueño*) and—since the central question is that of sexual knowledge—to the Garden of Eden, here delightfully transformed into the bucolic paradise of El Collado. But the modern experiment in educating a philosopher-prince also contains a thesis about contemporary Spanish sexual *mores* and the evil influence of the Church. A secondary theme of *Belarmino y Apolonio,* about how the World, the Flesh, and the Church combine to defile the purity of young love, is here viewed from a different angle. That is not to say, however, that Pérez de Ayala was turning into a moralising social realist in his middle age. *Luna de miel* and its sequel, although they have no verses, are more poetic than the *novelas poemáticas,* and exuberantly transform dull reality into a stylish artefact. The characters are splendidly unreal—archetypes, symbols, caricatures— and the action elegantly absurd.

Then, as might be expected, purely literary ingredients are mixed in, mainly just for fun. Don Cástulo conducts a running debate with himself about whether what is happening is Classical or

Romantic, tragic or comic, realistic or mythical. There are glances, as usual, in the direction of other literature: Dante, Goethe, Rousseau, and above all, in the title of the second part, the allusion to Cervantes's *Persiles y Sigismunda* which has been so often noted and so little studied or explained. In fact a close comparison of the two novels is revealing about the festive spirit of some of Pérez de Ayala's literary games, which so thoroughly exemplify some of the points on Ortega's list of the tendencies of modern art ('. . . a hacer que la obra de arte no sea sino obra de arte . . . a considerar el arte como juego y nada más . . . el arte . . . es una cosa sin trascendencia alguna . . .'). Pérez de Ayala reworks much of Cervantes's material, but only in the sense that many of the incidents of *Persiles* turn up, in a different order and changed form, in *Luna de miel* and *Los trabajos*. The basic situation between the pairs of lovers is obviously similar, and both books consider, in their different ways, the relationship between love and sex, but comparing the works does nothing to illuminate any obscure meaning in Pérez de Ayala's version, nor even to indicate how he interpreted Cervantes's rather enigmatic novel.

Tigre Juan and its sequel *El curandero de su honra* (1926) represent the summit of Pérez de Ayala's accomplishment in blending elements of reality and literature into a superb fiction. More profound and serious than *Luna de miel*, *Tigre Juan* draws on legend, art, folklore, psychoanalysis, and direct observation of life to make an absorbing novel which significantly uses musical terms to indicate the tempo of its chapters, for it is a work of great formal beauty and harmony. The Don Juan theme became a veritable obsession for writers of this period, but it was Leopoldo Alas, Pérez de Ayala's teacher at the University of Oviedo, who had first implied, in *La Regenta* of 1884, that the clue to Don Juan's behaviour may lie in his effeminacy. Pérez de Ayala developed the idea, drawing on Freudian findings to establish the theory, later taken up in the clinical analyses of Marañón, that Don Juan is the archetype of men with weak heterosexual urges and a strong sense of sexual insecurity which presses him constantly to prop up his feeble sexual desires with the stimulus of novelty. In *Tigre Juan,* the young Colás's analysis of Don Juan as a child who never grew up provides the further Freudian explanation that the nature of a man's first affair with a woman (his mother) affects all the others.

But *Tigre Juan,* as the title of its second part makes clearer, is more concerned with the opposite archetypal pole, Othello, or the

'Calderonian husband' who suspects—as Tigre Juan actually says—that all women except the Virgin Mary and his mother are innately indecent, and who therefore waits impatiently for his wife to betray him, premeditates his revenge, and when he imagines the fateful moment has arrived, expresses his profound, intense love and respect in a climactic act of murder. Juan's own effusive, tender embraces—of his late wife, the children in the market place, Colás, and Vespasiano—are all potentially murderous, as the victims often realise. A hazy perception of the fact even swims up into Juan's consciousness at the end of the novel. The role of the subconscious, both Freudian and Jungian, is very neatly incorporated into this tale of country life, not only in the series of subtle revelations which permit us to know the true personality of this gruff, complex-ridden woman-hater, but in sophisticated asides like the recognition of a father's maternal instincts, the age-old custom of the *covada*, and Juan's naïve attempt to simulate breast-feeding.

What impresses most in this fine novel, however, is not its exposition of archetypal polarities, nor its plumbing of psychological depths, but its superbly controlled orchestration of the parts. Although *Tigre Juan* mirrors reality more directly than any of Pérez de Ayala's novels since *Troteras y danzaderas*, it is nevertheless a poetic myth. A difficult balance and an improbable amalgam are triumphantly achieved, and most concisely represented in the character of Doña Iluminada: a very real person, worldly-wise, resigned to the reality which she perceives so much more clearly and deeply than anyone else in the novel, she is for all that a remote, mysterious, spiritualised essence of a woman, whose personality permeates the novel like a perfume or a melody. The same is true to a lesser extent of Colás and Herminia, characters whose essence is captured with the economy, precision, and dream-like vividness of good poetry. This is what gives the book its mythical quality. Although there are minor characters who afford the prosaic realism and knockabout comedy of real life, the major characters are distilled essences, who act and speak from the centre of their experience and leave out the irrelevant trimmings of life. The conversation between Herminia and Iluminada, for instance, when the latter decides that Herminia is woman enough to be Tigre Juan's wife, is not realistic. The inhabitants of Oviedo, or of any other real town, do not have the gift of refining their thoughts and emotions into quintessential dialogues of this kind. Yet they do not 'speak like a book'. Their talk is natural in a way that art can contrive but nature cannot copy. Liberated from the stumbling inarticulacies and evasions of real-life conversations and actions, the characters express only the true and significant kernels of their being. In this way, *Tigre Juan* and *El curandero de su honra* extract a poem from human reality, a poem which is genuinely present, but which needs the artifice of the poet to separate it from the insignificant dross which obscures it in real life.

There, with *Tigre Juan* and *El curandero de su honra,* ended the career of the novelist Pérez de Ayala, though he was only forty-six and seemed to be entering into the fullness of his mature creative powers, and though he lived for thirty-six more years. Nobody knows exactly why he wrote no more fiction. His life was busy enough in later years. His commitment to the Republican cause was rewarded with the post of ambassador to Britain, the Civil War drove him into exile in Argentina, but he soon returned to Madrid, where, like Baroja, he lived out his remaining years in the ambiguous position of a famous Spanish writer who had chosen to return to Franco's Spain, but who was famous for writings which were not favoured by the regime. In his last years he did a good deal of writing, but all of a very trivial kind—insipid Academician's articles for the first page of *ABC* and the like. It would appear that Pérez de Ayala was a lazy, comfort-loving man who readily accepted the fact that the novels he had written had not done very well in commercial terms, and who would have found it impossible anyway, after his return to Spain, to publish the kind of fiction he had written before the war, and so simply could not be bothered to persevere with the vocation that made him one of the major Spanish novelists of the twentieth century.

Gabriel Miró (1879-1930), although a year older than Pérez de Ayala, was slower in producing evidence of his remarkable talent. He contributed nothing to the literature of the Generation of 1898, and indeed his work up to the end of the first decade of the century is undistinguished. Miró himself repudiated what he had written before 1904, and it may be that if he had lived longer he would have eliminated more of his early writing from his authorised complete works. After half a dozen slight pieces, his publication of a more substantial novel, *Las cerezas del cementerio,* in 1910, marks something of a turning-point in his career. It is interesting to note that at the end of this novel the protagonist, Félix Valdivia, indulges in some moral and philosophical stocktaking which causes him to see things differently. At this moment we learn that 'había florecido dentro de su alma ese aroma que pincha y deja perfume de resignación, y se llama Ironía'. Although Miró had employed irony before 1910, the birth of an ironic vision in Félix's soul corresponds with a marked increase in Miró's use of it after *Las cerezas*.

Las cerezas nevertheless displays most of the features which Miró was to develop magnificently in his later work. The exultant intensity and luxuriance of his communication of beauty as perceived by all the senses, but particularly those of sight, smell, and taste, have been remarked on by all commentators. The same can be said of his prodigious linguistic artistry, his enormously rich vocabulary, and his Valencian regionalism. What is less often observed is that Miró's quest of beauty and happiness is accompanied by a preoccupation with ugliness and cruelty—usually expressed in gratuitously sadistic acts practised by humans on small and helpless animals. In *Las cerezas* Miró carefully makes the point that the brutal Alonso, who in the course of the novel kills or tortures a lizard, a fighting cock, a pigeon, a crippled idiot beggar, some flies, and a bat, is not some aberrant monstrosity, but the personification of a darker side of life which is inseparable from its totality. Not only do we learn that Alonso also once nursed a sick dog back to health with marvellous patience, but that Félix, the incarnation of aesthetic sensibility and the pursuit of joy, discovers in himself the same dark urges that prompt Alonso's brutality. In the prelude to the horrid incident of the man who bites the dog, and in his disappointment at finding that the poisoned 'vieja' is only an 'oveja', Félix remorsefully notes the pleasure he derives from cruel and savage emotions. Beauty is not truth for Miró. He does not flee from coarse reality in order to cloister and refine his perceptions in a private world of artifice. Once again the matter of perspective enters in. His artistic techniques aimed at transcending normal horizons of time and space will be considered presently, but as regards *Las cerezas*, perspective is important in a different sense. It is sometimes assumed that Félix speaks for Miró, but it is not so. The novel is about a young man whose sensitivity and thirst for beautiful experience distort his perception of reality, as he comes to realise just before his death. Nowhere is Miró more carefully and revealingly honest in this respect than in his treatment of 'la señora de Giner'. For most of the novel we see this woman through Félix's eyes, and so we are led to believe that she is an exquisitely romantic soul, tragically tied to a gross husband whom she loathes and fears. But after Félix dies, we get one devastating last glimpse of her, a rather stout, empty-headed housewife smiling affectionately at her husband, musing on how that queer young man had so insisted that she must be unhappy, and '. . . y con much ternura quitóle al marido las moscas que le chupaban en los lagrimales'. (*OC* 427.)[19]

The critical perspective in which Miró views his beauty-loving characters is even clearer in the case of Sigüenza, the central figure in three books of short, impressionistic anecdotes, descriptions, and memoirs—*Del vivir* (1904), *Libro de Sigüenza* (1917), *Años y leguas* (1928). Sigüenza has often been called Miró's *alter ego*; if he is, it does not prevent Miró using him constantly to show how enthusiasm for beautiful experiences can lead one into misinterpreting the world. Miró repeatedly brings Sigüenza down to earth, punctur-ing his fantasies, humorously, sadly, or violently. In 'Una tarde', for example, Sigüenza sets out to walk by the sea on a day of such perfect sunlit beauty that his thoughts turn to the purity and innocence of the Garden of Eden before the Fall. But in the course of his stroll he has to witness an appalling scene when some children deliberately drown their dog, watching its pitiful struggles with a chillingly innocent interest. They explain: 'lo atamos, para ver como se ahogaba un perro y todo lo que hacía', and the chapter ends: 'Y se quedaron mirando la paz y hermosura de la tarde, que eran como un perfume que llegaba a todos los corazones'. (*OC* 591). In 'Sigüenza, el pastor y el cordero', the order of events is reversed, for Sigüenza begins by being horrified by the butchering of a lamb, but ends by coming to realise that the splendid meal it then provided was a principal cause of the beatific serenity with which he contem-plates nature's beauty in the garden after dinner. Sigüenza certainly spends his life in search of beauty and joy, but when he does not find it, Miró tells us candidly what he does find.

Miró's ideas about his own writing, and the techniques he employed in his fiction, further emphasise the fact that his concern was much less to delight than to know and understand. In the many theoretical statements scattered through his work about his manner of contemplating the world, words like 'saber', 'interpretar', 'exac-titud', and 'realidad' are the important ones. Perspective is also employed as an aid to fuller understanding. For Miró, distance lends enchantment in a special sense. In the first place he notes that 'la dicha puede producirse por causas que, definidas concretamente, no son dichosas' (*OC* 649). This is evident in some of Sigüenza's experiences, but Miró goes further than the familiar truth that there is pleasure to be had from remembering sad moments in our past, and elaborates a more general theory of perception, best summed up in these words from *El humo dormido*:

> Hay episodios y zonas de nuestra vida que no se ven del todo hasta que los revivimos por el recuerdo; el recuerdo les aplica la plenitud de la conciencia; como hay emociones que no lo son del todo hasta que no reciben la fuerza lírica de la palabra, su palabra plena y exacta. (*OC* 692)

The experiences which Miró seeks to understand by applying to them the full, exact word will rarely be merely pleasant or beautiful.

The full and exact word itself will often have a symbolic function, particularly in Miró's two last great novels, *Nuestro Padre San Daniel* (1921) and *El obispo leproso* (1926), though the symbolism normally springs from natural conceptual relationships. For example, the second and third chapters of *Nuestro Padre* wish to establish the existence in Oleza of two attitudes to life which are to be fundamental to the story Miró is about to tell, and which are initially identified with the rival cults of San Daniel and the Virgin of El Moliner. To emphasise the antithesis, Miró makes use of a whole catalogue of pairs of antithetical images—dark–light, death–life, fear–love, sterility–fecundity, masculinity–femininity, force–grace, sin–innocence—and so on—skilfully introduced and sustained throughout the novels, and powerfully reinforcing the atmosphere Miró wishes to communicate, but also readily and easily intelligible to any reader. Miró's powers of evocation, however, and his communication of 'la plenitud de la conciencia', depend less on such large abstract images than on his admirable skill at selecting the detail which best defines and conjures up the totality of an experience. As Doctor Grifol of *Nuestro Padre* says: 'Creo que en el hombre, no es el conjunto moral ni el de su persona, sino una minucia, lo que puede guiarnos para conocerlo' (*OC* 881). Sometimes it is obvious which is the right 'minucia', as in the case of Nuño el Viejo's fur cap in *El humo dormido*, of which Miró remarks:

> Ver la gorra velluda en el perchero del vestíbulo era sentir a Nuño más cerca y más firmemente que si él la llevara.... El gorro de

Nuño el Viejo me ha explicado la razón y la fuerza evocadora de los símbolos y de muchos misterios. (*OC* 670)

But Miró's art is to select the details that most of us would miss, and then to dwell on them so that they divulge their full and exact significance. 'Nadie burle', says the wise Don Jesús of *El humo dormido,* 'de estas realidades de nuestras sensaciones donde reside casi toda la verdad de nuestra vida' (*OC* 698). What prompted Don Jesús to make this solemn injunction was simply his observation of that feeling of anxiety which possesses us when we momentarily lose something we had to hand a moment ago—and will eventually turn up, 'muy tranquilo, esperándonos'. His friend the Canon had been searching restlessly for his tobacco pouch. Don Jesús had noticed, but he did not offer his own, because the Canon did not want tobacco; he wanted to find his pouch.

The example is trivial, but it illustrates not only Miró's keen perception of small, revealing facets of 'la verdad de nuestra vida' but also his interest in the exact analysis of the 'minucia'. In his best writing he builds these details into patterns of general significance which makes serious and penetrating statements about the human condition. But seriousness does not preclude comic irony in Miró, and he often plays with the technique of the defining detail with ingenuity and humour. Sometimes he observes the way in which people will pay obtusely respectful attention to a supremely unrevealing 'minucia', like the 'heroic' big toe of the old man in *Nuestro Padre* who assisted in the brutal murder of the Conde de España (*OC* 795-6); sometimes ironic or incongruous details slyly reveal a character's true personality, as when Don Daniel Egea is reminded that he bears the name of the hero of the lions' den:

> . . . Y el señor Egea cruzaba valerosamente sus brazos, viéndose rodeado de feroces leones, enflaquecidos de hambre, que se le postraban y lamían desde las rodilleras hasta sus zapatillas de terciopelo malva, bordados por doña Corazón Motos, prima del hidalgo y dueña de un obrador de chocolates y cirios de la calle de la Verónica. (*OC* 790)

The idea, launched by Ortega's essay on *El obispo leproso* in 1927, that Miró is a mere formalist (whatever that may be) whose cult of beauty causes him to exclude from his work the action, ideas, and emotions which most people expect to find in prose fiction, will not

3 * *

bear a moment's serious examination, but it has been an unconscion-
able time dying. The only justification it has, and that inadequate, is
that a large part of Miró's output does not consist of novels, but of
the kind of short pieces that make up the Sigüenza books and *El
humo dormido*, to which must be added the *estampas* of the once
controversial, but minor, work *Figuras de la Pasión del Señor*
(1916-17) and of *El ángel, el molino, el caracol del faro* (1921).
After *Las cerezas del cementerio* of 1910, Miró published only four
novels, and one of these, *Niño y grande* (1922), had already appeared
in a slightly different form under the title of *Amores de Antón
Hernando* in 1909. So the only novels produced between the begin-
ing of Miró's mature period and his untimely death from peritonitis
at the age of fifty are *El abuelo del rey* (1915), *Nuestro Padre San
Daniel* (1921), and its sequel *El obispo leproso* (1926). These last
three novels alone suffice to demolish the myth of Miró's dehumanised
aestheticism and to secure his status as a major novelist. But it is not
even true that the *jornadas* and *estampas* of the other works confine
themselves to the communication of beauty. The first six pieces of
Libro de Sigüenza have the general title of 'Capítulos de la historia
de España', and express distinct, if ironic, attitudes on topics such
as politics, education, class, and religion in contemporary Spain. The
book also includes some moving human stories, notably the little
masterpiece 'La aldea en la ciudad', an immensely compassionate
and convincing tale of a day in the life of a humble, unsuccessful
rural priest.

The novels are principally about human behaviour and emotion
too. The brevity of *El abuelo del rey* does not prevent its being rich
in both. The lives of three generations of the Fernández-Pons family
are narrated in its brief compass, and the range of characters is a
very wide one, stretching from the tragic pathos of the first Agustín—
whose deranged passion for his dead wife illustrates one of Sigüenza's
observations on perspectives of time: that there are people of whose
existence we become truly aware only when they are dead or gone—
to the pure caricature of the bookworm Don César. Some of the
characters are realistic, but in the end the most important one
becomes the vanished and perhaps dead Agustín, whose weird
fictional existence is so real in its effect on the family as to convert
his grandfather into 'el abuelo del rey', and to bathe the town of
Sorosca in the reflection of his glory. *El abuelo del rey* is also a
thoughtful, humorous, and tender study of Spanish traditionalism.

Like *Nuestro Padre,* it chronicles a specific and important moment of change in Spanish provincial life, at the turn of the century, when the immemorial Sorosca of Don Arcadio's youth and of Don César's archives ('frío, oscuro, silencioso') finds itself having to retreat before the advance of La Marina, the modern quarter of the town, 'que se insolentaba entre la piedra arcaica, sufrida, venerable', as Miró says with the mixture of nostalgia and irony that always characterises his attitude to traditional provincial life. The last short chapter presents a deadpan account, largely in the language of the town hall, of the final collapse of the old city-walls before the arrival of the new road, linking the town—like the railway in *El obispo leproso*—with the modern world outside.

Obviously much of this anticipates the subject-matter of the two parts of Miró's last and greatest novel, which are about the same historically important moment of social change in this provincial capital peopled by 'capellanes y devotos', and again divided, as Miró ironically puts it, into 'dos mitades . . . la honesta y la relajada'. In this case the time of the action can be precisely dated, which is somewhat unusual in Miró, and therefore may be significant. Although Miró often mentions the time of year, and indicates the passing of time, his desire to achieve an evocatory effect by transcending immediate horizons of space and time normally leads him to conceal the exact date. His references are therefore usually only to cyclical time, to the weather of the month, to the liturgical calendar, or to the anniversary of some event remembered from the past. But a mention of Otero's attempt to assassinate the King fixes the action as taking place between April 1880 and the summer of 1897 (with an interval of eight years between the two parts of the novel). This, as we learn in *El obispo leproso*, was the period when the railway came—as a result of the Bishop's initiative—to the closed world of Oleza-Orihuela. Its symbolic importance is pointed at the end by the way it commutes the traditional life-sentence of women like the radiant Purita ('¡Ya no me quedo para vestir imágenes!'), but also leaves Don Magín, the fount of all that was best in old Oleza, a poignantly forlorn, dwindling figure on the station platform ('de lejos para siempre'). These were the years of Miró's childhood and early youth. Although his vision of old Oleza is deeply critical, one feels the force of his observation that a sad past may acquire great enchantment when evoked in memory. Furthermore, this is manifestly, for Miró, one of the 'episodes y zonas de nuestra vida que no se ven del todo hasta que los revivimos por el recuerdo'. Here is Miró exploiting memory in order to achieve 'la plenitud de la conciencia', an extremely sensitive and subtle reconstruction of a past that will never return.

But, of course, these remarkable novels are much more than scenes of provincial life, though the provincial and clerical setting is an important means of heightening the dramatic intensity of the main theme. This theme is the struggle between those who love life with a direct and innocent appetite for joy, and those sin-obsessed, life-hating ascetics who live in the dark behind closed shutters, victims of what Sigüenza called 'un sadismo contra su corazón peligroso para los demás' (OC 657). Although the characters who are most poisonously evil in human terms—Elvira, P. Bellod—are also the most pious in a conventional sense, the novels have no specific religious thesis. Don Magín, who is frankly in love with Purita, and the Bishop, who has thought tenderly of Paulina for years, are, together with the ridiculously innocent Don Jeromillo, the most truly Christian priests in Oleza.

Psychological studies of magnificent economy and power abound in the two books. Miró has a particular gift for showing how life makes people do what they do not want to do, or what they do not want to admit they are doing. In this respect the great passions of Pablo for María Fulgencia or of Paulina for her son are perhaps less interesting than the extraordinarily subtle portrayal of the raging inner fires that consume the granite-like Álvaro or his icy sister, or the deeply moving account of the destruction of poor, pitiful Don Daniel (like a small, helpless animal) by his self-righteous friends. The guilt-ridden sadists who have contrived to identify virtue and respectability with a masochistic denial of all innocent urges towards happiness are, however, defeated in the end. Or so it would seem. This part of the story is told in terms of a poetic myth, and through the symbol of the Bishop's leprosy. Like all good myths, this one is mysterious, and open to different interpretations. The most likely one seems to be offered by the naïve query of the Mother Superior of the Convent of the Visitación: '¿Y es lepra, lepra de verdad lo que aflige a su Ilustrísima?' '¡Y dicen que por los pecados de la diócesis!' (OC 1018). At the time of his death, all sorts of things reach their climax, and Paulina and Pablo return, after all, to the happiness of 'El Olivar'. As the bells toll for the man who has taken upon himself the guilt of Oleza, mother and son make the sign of the cross and set off, 'silenciosos, camino de la felicidad' (OC 1052).

The subdued and somewhat ambiguous ending to the novel suggests that Miró's conclusions, like his feelings about the passing of old Oleza, amount to something more complex than a mere account of the victory of one side in the struggle which has been the subject of the story. The reader is invited to do a good deal of thinking for himself. But it would seem that what the Bishop's martyrdom wins for Oleza is wisdom rather than victory. The novel's earlier polarity of innocence and evil is now tempered by understanding. Elvira, Álvaro, and Amancio end by commanding pity rather than contempt and anger. Paulina and Pablo go off silent, reflective, on the road to happiness, but possibly still far from their destination. They have learnt that following their natural impulses does not necessarily produce happiness. They have suffered and caused others to suffer. Perhaps this is the ultimate significance of the Bishop's example. He, too, loved life with a pure and spontaneous joyfulness; life responded by inflicting on him a loathsome, disfiguring disease. Yet the disease never reached his soul, and by enduring it steadily he was able to play his part in bringing to Oleza and its inhabitants a civilised maturity and serenity which they had formerly lacked.

The work of the five novelists considered so far is what makes the first three decades of the twentieth century an outstanding period for Spanish prose fiction. In such distinguished company, other able and interesting writers of the time can only receive brief mention.

Azorín (José Martínez Ruiz, 1873-1967) is a major figure in the history of Spanish letters, the inventor and most indisputable member of the Generation of 1898, whose literature he enriched with the early trilogy of novels.[20] But after 1904 his contribution to prose fiction is mainly of a marginal kind. He wrote no more novels for many years, but produced instead a great many examples of the kind of book for which he is best known: collections of short, reflective sketches of Spanish life, where description is mixed with history, literary reminiscence, and Azorín's own imaginings. La ruta de don Quijote (1905), Los pueblos (1905), España (1909), Castilla (1912), El paisaje de España visto por los españoles (1917), and Una hora de España (1924) are only a few of the most famous titles from a long list of works in which Azorín beats a steady retreat from his youthful iconoclasm and reformism into conservatism and traditionalism, and develops a vision of Spain where consolation becomes more important than truth. There is a good deal of fiction in these works, for although Azorín invariably takes a real place, or historical character or moment, or work of literature, as his starting-point, his imagination then roams freely in a world of his own creation, where past and present are intertwined, historical characters meet fictional ones, and the fictional ones are sometimes Azorín's inventions, sometimes somebody else's, but most characteristically a blend of the two. This last tendency, to tell his own stories about famous fictional figures, can be irritating and confusing when it creeps into his more specifically literary studies. But when his aim is purely to capture in an aesthetic experience some aspect of traditional Spanish life, the merging of such elements can be extremely evocative.

These prose pieces give a curious and consistent impression of smallness. Their purpose is very modest. Although there are references to great events and famous personages, Azorín's horror of any kind of grandiloquence makes him concentrate on the humble and the commonplace, and his vision, even if he is describing a whole broad Castilian landscape, is composed of a few sharply defined details. Everything is brief in these books: their chapters of a page or two, their sentences, even their words. For Azorín, simplicity and clarity were, at least at this period, the beginning and end of a good style. Although he said, in *Una hora de España* (Chapter 11), that 'lo primero en el estilo es la claridad', he did not go on, in theory or in practice, to any secondary consideration. While Valle-Inclán, Pérez de Ayala, and Miró were enriching the language of literature, Azorín was only concerned with making it clearer and simpler.

In 1922 Azorín began writing novels again, though in his *Don Juan* of that year the change was hardly perceptible. It has no plot, no interest in individual character, no ideological content, and is merely a further series of descriptions, anecdotes from the past and present, and glimpses of some of the inhabitants of a small Castilian town. It is only the town which gives the fragments any unity. The only feature of *Don Juan* that was not present in the essays is an apparently mischievous attempt to mystify the reader. Incongruous details which clamour for explanation are left unexplained, like the provocatively named Doctor Quijano, normal in all respects except that he receives visits from an invisible being. The allusions to the Don Juan legend also belong in this category, and this remains true of Azorín's next novel, *Doña Inés* (1925), whose title suggests that it, too, will have something to do with the legend, but which is again a series of static fragments strung together in incongruous fashion.

Don Juan has a prologue and an epilogue which describe him as a great sinner who was saved, yet the nearest he comes to sin in the novel is a fleeting moment of attraction for the young Jeanette (whose father, however, is El Maestre Don Gonzalo). Similarly Doña Inés, who is nothing like the shy child of *Don Juan Tenorio,* nevertheless receives a letter which has a marked emotional effect on her, but we never learn who sent it or what it says. Such inconsequential half-allusions to Zorrilla's work—and there are others—are so mysterious as to suggest that Azorín's purpose is to be deliberately meaningless.

The preface to his next novel, *Félix Vargas* (1928; later retitled *El caballero inactual*), proclaims a new literary aim of abolishing 'organic' relationships or connections formed between objects and people by space, time, and logic; the novel tells the story of a man who lives in three different centuries, and in different parts of France and Spain, at the same time, and whose world is populated by real and fictional characters. The same principles appear to govern *Superrealismo* (1929; later retitled *El libro de Levante*). But the principles are neither surrealistic nor new in Azorín's writing. What he does is to assert as a literary theory, and to carry to extravagant extremes, his long-standing practice of fusing past and present, fact and fiction, into a new literary artefact. Perhaps it was his way of affirming, in his middle fifties and in the century's gay twenties, that he could be as avant-garde as the next man. Although the experiment is not without historical interest as another of the period's attempts to supersede conventional realism, it lacks the coherent purpose of Valle-Inclán's or Pérez de Ayala's explorations of new formal possibilities. One cannot escape the uncomfortable feeling that Azorín does not really know what he is doing, particularly when he calls one of his new-style novels *Superrealismo;* for there is no question of his drawing on material furnished by the subconscious or the world of dreams, and the title seems to be merely a fashionable sort of apology for having taken liberties with traditional novelistic forms.

After the Civil War Azorín lived on to a great age in Madrid as a revered relic of the past. He continued to write books of essays about traditional Spain, but he also wrote a few more novels, such as *Capricho* (1942), *La isla sin aurora* (1944), and *Salvadora de Olbena* (1944). These novels constitute an ironic kind of anachronism. While young Spanish novelists were returning to the social moralising and realistic techniques of the late nineteenth century, the seventy-year-old Azorín's highly unrealistic novels continued to assert the need for art to differ from reality. They still experiment with perspective, demolish reality's laws of space, time, and character, and recreate life in more aesthetically interesting patterns. They did not please a public which had returned to the view that the business of art is to mirror life. Azorín has continued to be esteemed as the great painter of the eternal Spanish landscape. But the years immediately after an author's death tend to be a poor guide as to how posterity will judge him, particularly if he has been very well known for a very long time, and it is not impossible that in due course Azorín's late experiments with the art of fiction will be found to merit as much attention as his nostalgic evocations of Spain's past.

It is less likely that time will bring any great revival of interest in the writings of Ramón Gómez de la Serna (1888-1963), who impressed his extravagant, colourful personality on the literary world of his day with such force that in reminiscences and studies of the period he is still referred to simply as 'Ramón'. But the Civil War destroyed that world, and drove Ramón to Buenos Aires, where he lived out his remaining years in uncharacteristic obscurity. His great fame has now dwindled to what seems more realistic proportions, those of a writer of considerable ingenuity and originality who squandered his talents in too much writing of too many kinds—novels, stories, essays, articles, memoirs, a few plays—all stamped by his own determined frivolity and exuberant disorderliness. But in spite of the diversity of his literary activity, he is most often remembered for his so-called *greguerías*. Gómez de la Serna's claim to have invented the *greguería* evidently afforded him deep satisfaction, to judge by the way he constantly added to his *post facto* theorising about it in successive editions and selections of the thousands of examples he produced. To what extent the cult of the brilliant, surprising metaphor in Spanish poetry and prose of the twenties derived from Gómez de la Serna has often been debated. Although on the one hand he claimed to have invented the *greguería* in 1910, Gómez de la Serna himself admitted that writers had cultivated the genre, or something like it, at least since the days of the Caliphate of Córdoba. What is less debatable is its central importance to all his own work, including his novels and essays. According to his theory, the *greguería* is metaphor plus humour, a witty, explosive perception of the relationship between one thing and another. In fact a glance at any few pages of *greguerías* shows them to be of mixed character. Sometimes there is a suggestion of surrealism—'La calavera es un reloj muerto'—sometimes they merely attempt a striking association of small details of reality with hardly any element of fantasy—'Los porteros leen el periódico como si estuviesen enterándose de los chismes de vecindad'—and all too often they are only insipid Christmas-cracker jokes—'La T es el martillo del abecedario', 'El mar debía tener un agujerito por donde irse desaguando'. What they have in common is their remorseless triviality. Even the most daring or poetic of them seem to be constrained by the fear that someone will accuse their author of having produced something truly penetrating or beautiful.

This apparent fear gives unity to Gómez de la Serna's varied literary output. So seriously does he maintain his view that life is utterly unserious that his cult of gay absurdity becomes almost morbidly nihilistic and cynical. In the preface to the 1941 edition of one of his earliest novels, *El doctor inverosímil* (1914; but much amplified in later editions), he makes the typically bold claim of having been the first to introduce techniques of Freudian analysis into Spanish prose fiction. But the book is a completely frivolous series of expanded *greguerías*. The improbable doctor succeeds by diagnosing, for instance, in the case of a patient who is mysteriously dying, 'No hay nada que conserve la corrupción como unos guantes de cabritilla demasiado anticuados', and prescribing that the gloves should be thrown away; the patient returns to perfect health. *Greguerías* are frequently incorporated into the narrative of his novels; the slight plot of *El secreto del acueducto* (1922), for example, is barely more than a pretext for a stream of epigrammatic reflections on the aqueduct of Segovia.

The relationship between life and art in Gómez de la Serna's mature novels reveals clearly that he is yet another victim of *angustia vital* who has taken refuge in art as a consequence. The stories he tells tend to be sordid and pessimistic, particularly when they are about love and sex. The spectre of death increasingly casts its shadow over meaningless, unhappy lives. And for all his determination to escape from the squalid reality of human existence into trivial artifice, Gómez de la Serna is drawn into the business of interpreting that reality. One of his best novels, *El novelista* (1923), although it still seeks to escape from life's unpleasant truths by playing the game of the *greguería*, also considers, in much the same way as *Belarmino y Apolonio*, the question of different ways of looking at human experience. Like Pérez de Ayala's book, *El novelista* is a novel about how to write novels, and the protagonist takes perspectivism to the down-to-earth extreme of renting flats in different parts of Madrid and writing differently in each of them, in order to combine multiple points of view in his vision of the life of the city. Even those of Gómez de la Serna's novels which seem to offer a strong story and material drawn from raw reality, like *El torero Caracho* (1926), drift off all the time into the deliberate transformation of such unpalatable material into a more tolerable artifice, and continue to celebrate the act of observation for its own sake, or for the sake of affirming that the game of art is a blessed relief from the burden of life.

In his last novels, particularly *Las tres gracias* (1949) and *Piso bajo* (1961; but with a preface dated 1957), stories of life in a vanished Madrid that lived on in the imagination of an old man on the other side of the Atlantic, Gómez de la Serna reveals more clearly than before to what extent his art had been the product of a deeply pessimistic outlook on life. These are melancholy works, and if *Piso bajo,* his last novel, seeks to salvage some illusions of idealism and happiness from experience, it also contains the painful awareness that 'la vida es la más profunda desapariencia, todo en ella es verdad, demasiado verdad'. On its last page is Gómez de la Serna's last *greguería,* referring to the strange and solitary life of the scientist Pedro Savedra, dedicated to discovering the ultimate mysteries of the atom: 'Su vida había sido atrevida, pero siempre entre Dios y la muerte, dándose cuenta de que el hombre está entre paréntesis de muertos'.

Gómez de la Serna's exact contemporary Benjamín Jarnés (1888-1949) was also very much a man of his times, and since the literature of those times is at present out of favour, he is little read today. But whereas Gómez de la Serna's fame still rests precariously on fading memories of his picturesque personality, Jarnés lived out his life as an obscure civil servant, and is remembered, if at all, only for what he wrote. But what he wrote, even if it is not to contemporary taste, is more substantial than what Gómez de la Serna wrote, and nearer to the achievements of his great contemporaries.

As a regular contributor to Ortega's *Revista de Occidente,* and a modish literary critic of the twenties, alert to all the latest experiments of European art, it was only to be expected that Jarnés's own fiction should treat reality as raw material to be broken down and refashioned into a new and different experience. Another crime of which modern taste holds him guilty is that he was a superb stylist, who gloried in the capacity of language to explore, embellish, and make fun of life. He is not much concerned either with getting on with an interesting story or giving a straightforward, recognisable description of the circumstances of everyday life. Jarnés is indeed another writer whose reworking of familiar stories and literary themes serves to remind us that it is far from his purpose to copy life. Apart from his semi-fictional biographies such as *Sor Patrocinio* (1929) and *Zumalacárregui* (1931), his *San Alejo* (1928) retells a legend well known to Spaniards, as does *Viviana y Merlín* (1929), in which the author and Vivien agree that Tennyson's version is a calumny. *Teoría del zumbel* (1930) relies heavily on *Don Quixote* to make its points, and the scenes of *Escenas junto a la muerte* (1931) are all variations on literary themes, including an interesting new version of *El alcalde de Zalamea* as a film, with a sad, romantic Charlie Chaplin added to the original cast; *Lo rojo y lo azul*, in case the title's allusion is not plain enough, is subtitled 'Homenaje a Stendhal'.

Comparison of Jarnés with Miró is inescapable. As well as an elaborately cultivated style with a wealth of concise, poetic metaphor and symbol, and a concern to extract the last ounce of significance from small details of experience, Jarnés shares Miró's joyful celebration of sensual pleasure and suspicion of any sort of asceticism, from San Alejo's religious masochism to the life-denying neoplatonism of King Arthur's court—we learn ominously that Plotinus is one of Merlin's favourite authors. In *El convidado de papel* (1928), senseless repression of innocent joy is expressly associated with both the Church and contemporary bourgeois ideas of respectability.

But in other respects, Jarnés's work bears a surprising resemblance to Unamuno's. From about 1928 onwards, many of his characters wonder and worry about who they are, what constitutes their distinctive identity. One of San Alejo's reasons for fleeing from his aristocratic home and his lovely bride is that the predictability of his life seems to him to mean anonymity. *Locura y muerte de nadie* (1929) is about the efforts of a Juan Sánchez to acquire a distinct identity-for-others, as a great thief, a great cuckold, a person of illustrious descent, anything that will make him memorable. But all in vain; people still confuse him with Juan Martínez, and when he is run over by a lorry his death is reported as that of 'a pedestrian'. An epilogue stresses the total absence in the world thereafter of any sign that he ever passed through it. *Teoría del zumbel,* which includes Unamuno-like confrontations between the author and rebellious characters, and a girl who at the start of the novel is empty of identity because she has never had to choose a course of action, considers the possibility of changing one's identity by an act of will. *Escenas junto a la muerte* is so called because the protagonist has been so severely shocked by the spectacle of his own personality—which he refers to as 'el otro'—that he tries to commit suicide. A further aspect of the problem of authentic existence is explored in *Lo rojo y lo azul,* in Julio's obsession with the idea that most of us deprive our lives of meaning by living each moment not for its own sake, but as a preparation for something in the future.

It is quite evident that Jarnés is deeply concerned with the meaning and quality of real life, and that in this sense his novels are the very reverse of 'dehumanised'. But his artistic manner conforms closely to Ortega's observations about the tendencies of modern art. To say what his novels are 'about' is to mention one of their least important features. Like Miró again, he dwells absorbingly on the act of observation itself, and the fragments of reality which serve as pretexts for his experiments in fiction are usually very trivial. The beginning of the first of the *Escenas junto a la muerte* provides a good example. Our hero, the humble 'opositor número 7', sits in a library, extracting boring notes from a history book and observing a pretty girl who from the book on her desk would appear to be a medical student, though she is actually occupied in writing a letter. Jarnés builds these sparse materials into an impressively entertaining display of his creative and stylistic powers which reminds one of Joyce in festive mood. His techniques are much closer to those of contemporary poetry than of traditional prose fiction; it is not relevant to inquire what, in plain words, he means to say nor what, in terms of mere narrative, is going on. At the start of the fourth chapter of *Teoría del zumbel*, for instance, Saulo undergoes a series of experiences which on close inspection turn out to be those of a car crash. The facts could have been narrated explicitly in a few sentences, the action is a matter of minutes, and even Saulo's mental sensations could have been recorded comprehensively in a paragraph or two, but Jarnés devotes eight pages of his short novel to what constitutes an ambitious prose poem about a motor accident.

Although this kind of prose poetry is the essence of his originality and artistry, Jarnés's later novels reveal a tendency to move away from it in the direction of a more conventional style of narration. Whether the change represents a loss or a gain for literature will doubtless remain a matter of opinion; the later work, although more similar to the kind of fiction which many people have written, is still very good. The change took place quite quickly. The difference between, for example, *Paula y Paulita* of 1929 and *Lo rojo y lo azul* of 1932, is quite marked. The earlier work has practically no action, and takes place in the dreamy atmosphere of a quiet spa, whereas *Lo rojo* is set in a very real atmosphere of contemporary Barcelona and Saragossa, and deals directly with such unpoetic subjects as differences in social class, the hard life of girls on the edge of prostitution, and an abortive attempt at a revolutionary *coup* by workers and soldiers in Saragossa. The characters of the latter novel have become thoroughly human in comparison with their predecessors in Jarnés's works. In *Teoría del zumbel* the author had informed the creatures of his fiction that they were not really characters at all. The real characters of his novel, he said, were 'un zumbel, un reloj, un telegrama'—symbols which feature prominently in the book, and which are related to remarks in the preface about conscious and subconscious (personal and collective) experience. The shadowy personages of the novel are therefore no more than objects which Jarnés uses for experimental purposes in this subtle and intelligent parable of the motivation of human behaviour. But in *Lo rojo* the characters are real people, observed with brilliant wit and humour, who elicit responses of compassion, derision, identification. The novel ends by communicating Jarnés's dismay at the prospect of the murderous political divisions already apparent in the early thirties, and with a strong plea—in the very human account of Julio's failure to do his political duty—for solutions to Spain's social and political problems that do not require the killing of good men.

After this novel, Jarnés, like many other writers, became more and more directly involved in politics. Then came the war, which for him meant exile, and failing health. Though he wrote a little more, there is every sign that his case was one of many where political events deprived Spain of the best work of a writer who was approaching the height of his powers.

The best and most interesting novels of this period are inspired, except in Baroja's case, by the conviction that it is the function of art to turn dull and incoherent reality into something more meaningful or more attractive. But this naturally did not mean that the traditional novel of anecdote and description ceased to exist, nor even that its popularity waned at this time. Some mention must finally be made, therefore, of the kind of authors whose works were actually read in Spain. One of the most widely read of all continued to be Vicente Blasco Ibáñez (1867-1928). His best work, represented by strong social novels like *La barraca* (1898), *Cañas y barro* (1902), and *La bodega* (1905), was finished by the end of the first decade of the century, but he went on turning out new books until his death. His aggressively anti-German novels of the European war, *Los cuatro jinetes del Apocalipsis* (1916), *Mare nostrum* (1917), and the historical novels of his last years, *El papa del mar* (1925) and *A los pies de Venus* (1926), were all best-sellers. Blasco's own earlier naturalist tendencies were carried on in the novels of Felipe Trigo (1865-1916), Eduardo Zamacois (1876-   ), and Pedro Mata (1875-1946), which did well on a reputation for being mildly pornographic, but the best of them—Trigo's *El médico rural* (1912), Zamacois's *La opinión ajena* (1913) and *El delito de todos* (1933), contain much sharp, leftish social criticism. More firmly committed still is the social realism of Manuel Ciges Aparicio (1873-1936) in novels like *Villavieja* (1914) and his last and best book, *Los caimanes* (1931). The ideals of the other ideological extreme were upheld by the immensely popular Ricardo León (1877-1943), ultra-conservative and Catholic, rabidly traditionalist and not shy of saying so in such aggressive thesis novels as *Casta de hidalgos* (1908) and *El amor de los amores* (1917). A less demented nostalgia for the genteel values of a vanishing age forms part of the subject-matter of Concha Espina (1877-1955). Some of her novels are rather watery accounts of the lives of sentimental, spiritual, but very ordinary young ladies such as one imagines Concha Espina to have been—*La niña de Luzmela* (1909), *La rosa de los vientos* (1916). But other novels have an unexpectedly strong element of social comment. *La esfinge maragata* (1914), although its main plot is still novelettish, takes a frank and searching look at the miseries of life in the province of León, and *El metal de los muertos* (1920), by far her best book, is a truly shocking record of the dreadful conditions of life and work in the Río Tinto mines of Huelva (though she changes the names), and is fired by an indignation which only just stops short of making it a socialist thesis.

The one genuinely popular writer who departed from the techniques of realistic anecdote was Wenceslao Fernández Flórez (1884-1964), although he was in every sense a conservative and a great mocker of avant-garde and minority art. His political satires, during and after the Republic—*Una isla en el mar rojo* (1938), *La novela número 13*

(1941)—his unequivocal support of the Franco regime, and the regime's approval of him as one of the few literary lions to have seen the light all along, often turn critical opinions of him, one way or the other, into political manifestos. But until the thirties the substance of his satire was more social than political. Fernández Flórez objected, with some justification, to being classified as a mere humorist. His work has the fairly serious aim of commenting on human weakness and folly. Sometimes he does this in a realistic manner—*Volvoreta* (1917), *Ha entrado un ladrón* (1920)—but he shows more ingenuity in allegorical fantasies like *El secreto de Barba Azul* (1923), and his most famous novel, *Las siete columnas* (1926). The latter works out in a way that the men of the Enlightenment would have appreciated, the thesis that the seven deadly sins are the basis of the stable, civilised society we know and love. Behind the fantasy there may be an intention to deride the utopian view of human nature which underlies Anarchist thinking (the 'withdrawal' of the sin of avarice in the novel, for example, results in a total collapse of agriculture and industry), but in general Fernández Flórez is more concerned with psychology than with politics, and his allegory presents an acceptable gloss on the absurdity of the human condition, with which any of the major writers of the period would surely have agreed.

Fernández Flórez was one of the few Spanish writers whose work was not seriously affected by the Civil War and the new regime. For most of them the war meant the end of an epoch, for some, the end of their serious work, for a few, the end of their lives. The handful of important novelists who were old enough to have contributed to the best prose fiction of this period, but also young enough, or resilient enough, to take the blow of exile in their stride, so that their work cannot be characterised as belonging to either the pre-war or post-war period, will be considered separately.

NOTES

1. See Donald L. Shaw, *A Literary History of Spain: The Nineteenth Century*, pp. 159 ff.
2. Ibid., pp. 171-2.
3. Cf. C. Blanco Aguinaga, *El Unamuno contemplativo* (Mexico, 1959).
4. See J. Alberich, 'Cara de Plata, fuera de serie', BHS, XLV (1968), 299-308.
5. J. Rubia Barcia, 'The Esperpento: a New Novelistic Dimension', *Valle-Inclán Centennial Studies* (Austin, Texas, 1968).

6. See A. Zamora Vicente, *La realidad esperpéntica* (Madrid, 1969), pp. 22-61.

7. See Jean Franco, 'The Concept of Time in *El ruedo ibérico*', *BHS*, XXXIX (1962), 177-87.

8. Ibid.

9. See Emma Susana Speratti-Piñero, *De 'Sonata de otoño' al esperpento* (London, 1968), *passim*.

10. For Baroja's contribution to the collective *Weltanschauung* of Spanish intellectuals during the early part of the century see Shaw, op. cit., pp. 166-71.

11. See Shaw, op. cit., pp. 166-7, and D. L. Shaw, 'A Reply to "Deshumanización": Baroja on the Art of the Novel', *HR*, XXV (1957), 105-11.

12. See G. Marañón, *Obras completas* (Madrid, 1966-), I, xvi.

13. See S. H. Eoff, *The Modern Spanish Novel* (London, 1962), p. 173.

14. Pío Baroja, *Memorias* (Madrid, 1955), p. 1217.

15. See Shaw, *A Literary History of Spain*, p. 167.

16. Ibid., pp. 173-6.

17. Preface to *Troteras y danzaderas* (Buenos Aires, 1942), p. 19.

18. Preface to *Poesías completas* (Buenos Aires, 1942), p. 14.

19. OC references are to pages in G. Miró, *Obras completas* (4th edn., Madrid, 1961).

20. Shaw, op. cit., pp. 164-5.

Chapter 2

POETRY

AN AGE WHOSE BEST LITERATURE is written by and for a cultivated minority is likely to be a propitious one for poetry, and the first four decades of the twentieth century are as brilliant a period for Spanish poetry as they are for prose literature. The century came in on the crest of the wave of *modernismo*. Unlike the idea of the 'Generation of 98', *modernismo* is not a term thought up by literary historians looking back on the period. At the turn of the century, a group of young writers who called themselves *modernistas* engaged in a vigorous crusade of protest and reform, and dedicated themselves for some years to collective literary activities—magazines, meetings, manifestos—under the modernist banner. It was only later, when *modernismo* was no longer a battle-cry and its products had become respectable in Spain, that they began to be more aware of what distinguished them from each other, and later still that critics began to try to define the essence of *modernismo* and to separate it from other literary trends of the time.

The process of definition is still going on. It is, however, evident that *modernismo* was, among other things, a resurgence of the anguish that characterised European Romantic literature, which seemed for a time to have been put to flight by the self-confidence of nineteenth-century faith in scientific rationalism. The anguish had deep philosophical roots, reaching down to the death of God and the disappearance of all that his presence had once guaranteed; the new poetry often points to this in its brooding on themes of vanished childhood, lost paradises, old, ordered, enclosed gardens. The *modernistas*, like the Romantics, not only recognised the cruel absurdity of human life in general, but bore a special grudge against the epoch into which it had been their misfortune to be born, an ugly, materialistic, philistine age where the Artist was an outcast. Their response was to affirm that it was the mission of art to supply the meaning and beauty which life lacked.

Like the rest of their generation, the *modernistas* were contemptuous of the literature of the immediate past, which had asserted faithful representation of reality as an artistic aim, and had exalted the realist novel as a model of artistic achievement. *Modernismo,* as its name implies, meant breaking with all this and doing new things in new ways. In modernist poetry, new subjects, new techniques, metres, vocabulary, flourished as they had never managed to do in the Romantic period.

Modernismo was also self-consciously cosmopolitan. Its practitioners felt they were taking part, perhaps somewhat belatedly, in a revolution of sensibility that was not confined to Spain or even Europe, but whose centre was indisputably Paris. Whether or not Spanish writers needed the Nicaraguan Rubén Darío to call their attention to the importance of recent French poetry, from Hugo to the Symbolists, by 1900 poets were drawing inspiration directly from France, and except in matters of form, Spanish *modernismo* may owe more to Verlaine than to Darío.

The importance to Spanish literature of Darío's *Azul* (1888) and *Prosas profanas* (1896) is not, of course, to be denied. These books helped to create a new kind of poetry in Spanish. But their effect was rather to liberate Spanish poets from old inhibitions than to provide a model to be copied. In this respect, the historical quibble about whether Darío or the Spanish poet Salvador Rueda initiated the *modernista* movement in Spain, though unimportant in itself, throws some light on poetic developments at the turn of the century.

Rueda (1857-1933) began publishing books of verse in 1883, five years before the appearance of *Azul*. His poetry reveals a clear desire to break with the formulas of the eighties, and to return to the pursuit of beauty, colour, and harmony. Its metrical innovations, which do in fact anticipate some of Darío's, were later to be the basis of Rueda's claim that he, and not Darío, was the father of *modernismo*. Rueda also undoubtedly exercised some influence on young Spanish poets. But his own poetry obviously lacks many of the elements normally associated with *modernismo*. Although he wrote poems about swans and lilies, they are, like the rest of his work, descriptions or meditations on what he sees before him, and contain none of the magic and mystery of modernist inventions. A favourite anthology piece is his description of a water-melon. He also hymns the virtues of bread. More fundamentally, he is broadly content with the world as he finds it. He is fond and proud of Spain, especially his native Andalusia, which he extols in a naïve and superficial way that no self-respecting poet of Jiménez's generation would have permitted himself. The fact is that Rueda, a comparatively uncultured and unsophisticated poet, was reflecting in his own way the beginning of the new poetic sensibility which doubtless would have found expression in Spain without his or Rubén Darío's help, although both of them pointed the way towards the kind of poetry that younger poets wanted to write.

The poetry that young Spanish poets began to produce at the beginning of the century immediately differed from Darío's in several respects, so that the term *modernismo* must be allowed a fairly wide sense if it is to refer both to Darío and to the early work of the Machado brothers, Villaespesa, Jiménez, and Valle-Inclán. The difference is sometimes exaggerated. It is true that Spanish writers (with the exception of Valle-Inclán in the *Sonatas*) tended to reject the exotic external trappings of Darío's poems, his sensuous communication of beauty and the virtuoso musicality of his language. But there is more to Darío than this. He was from the start a symbolist at least in the broad sense that his poetry aims at creating a 'state of mind', and at capturing the essences that lie beneath the changing surface of things. His purpose is not to describe things because they are beautiful, but to evoke the feelings they inspire. His swans on their azure lakes, for instance, are not made of feathers, but—as he says in 'Blasón'—of perfume, ermine, white light, silk, and dreams.

On the other hand, Spanish poets turned inwards in a way that Darío rarely did, and if they often used techniques suggested to them by reading *Azul* and *Prosas profanas*, they applied them to the creation of a sad, uncertain, introspective poetry very unlike most of Darío's. The influence of Bécquer was beginning to make itself felt. The title of Manuel Machado's first book was *Alma*, that of Jiménez's, *Almas de violeta*, and of Antonio Machado's *Soledades*; the flood of poetry produced by Villaespesa at this period is full of intimate confession and self-pity, and reminds one more of Espronceda than of anything in *Prosas profanas*. Villaespesa (1866-1936), however, wrote in a manner very different from that of the Spanish Romantics; his poetry, perhaps because of his limited poetic gifts, demonstrates more clearly than that of his greater contemporaries its direct debt to France. Luis Cernuda rightly calls Villaespesa 'el puente por donde el modernismo pasa a una nueva generación de escritores',[1] and it is a bridge built out of French materials. Darío's 'visiones de países lejanos o imposibles', his princesses and centaurs, rarely appear. Instead we have melancholy mood-landscapes, dimmed by the dying light of evening or by sad autumnal rain, and the persistent 'parque viejo' with its roses, dark avenues of trees, and murmuring or weeping fountains—the 'jardín de mis recuerdos', as Villaespesa calls it in one poem. All this is evoked with the 'mot vague' of Verlaine's 'Art poétique', in order to convey not a scene but a feeling about it. Villaespesa's wish to 'pintar flores, no como son, y sí como las vemos' may not be so well phrased as Mallarmé's famous statements, but it is obviously to the same effect. The trouble is that his poetic intuitions are neither deep nor subtle, and rarely strike a responsive note of recognition or discovery in the reader. His most typical poems merely stare out at the dusk or the rain, or brood on half-forgotten gardens, and feel very sad. Two lines of his 'Balada de la saudade y el corazón' provide an apt summary of all his poetry. The heart has been asked how to define Portuguese 'saudade', and the poem ends: 'Y el corazón, no sabiendo/qué contestar, suspiró . . .' Villaespesa played a significant personal part in helping to launch other young poets, notably Jiménez, on their poetic careers, but his own poems have not stood the test of changing taste, and he is little read today.

Something like the same oblivion, but for different reasons and with less justice, has been the fate of Manuel Machado (1874-1936). The reasons include the irrelevant one that the reputation of his younger brother Antonio overshadows his own, the fact that most of his best work was done very early in his life, and the disrepute he came under in some quarters for his support for Primo de Rivera's dictatorship, and more importantly, for Franco's cause, on whose behalf he wrote some embarrassing propagandist poems. Such factors have reduced Machado in the opinion of many to the stature of a minor poet, the author of a handful of fine poems, but whose apathy led him into aesthetic escapism when other poets were doing more important things.

The principal injustice of this idea of Manuel Machado is that it ignores the impressive, if unequal, range of his poetic output and talents. His first and best book of poems, *Alma* (1902), reveals a wide variety of skills. By the time he wrote it he was well known in the literary world, and he had spent two years in Paris, where he had extended his literary horizons and acquired the self-confidence to write whatever he felt like writing. Some of the poems of *Alma* explore, often with striking symbols, the theme suggested by the book's title, an inner world of deep longings, hopes, and fears, delving deeply into the same corridors of the mind which his brother Antonio was roaming at this period. *Alma*'s profound existential pessimism is quite as serious as that of Antonio's better known *Soledades*. *Alma* also includes the first and most famous of Machado's attempts to convey in a poem the impression given by a painting, 'Felipe IV'. The experiment had been made by a number of French poets before him, but he was the first Spanish exponent of this kind of evocative verse portraiture, of which he produced many fine examples. A different kind of evocation of a past age, also in *Alma*, is 'Castilla', a vivid version of an incident in the Poem of the Cid. The contrast between the robust descriptive force of this poem and the languid subtlety of 'Felipe IV' gives a good idea of the versatility of Machado's poetic capacities at this time.

Two further styles enrich the variety of Machado's art. *Alma* also provides examples of his interest in making poetry out of Andalusian folklore (for which his father's collections and those of Agustín Durán, to whom his family was related, provided much material), which was to occupy him more in later years and was to find echoes in the work of later poets like Lorca and Alberti. Another string to his bow, and an original one as far as Spanish literature was concerned, was his poetry about the misery and squalor of modern city life, which he expresses principally in the cruel, 'anti-poetic' verses of *El mal poema* (1909).

In 1910, not long after publishing *El mal poema*, he married his cousin and childhood sweetheart Eulalia Cáceres, and changed his way of life. Although he continued to be a prominent figure—much more so than his brother—in the social and literary world, and to write poetry, even, occasionally, good poems, the quality of his work after his marriage declined even more markedly than its quantity. People continued to read his poetry. The collection of Andalusian poems, *Cante hondo*, of 1912, was one of his most financially successful volumes of verse. But he was already becoming a respected figure of the past. His last years were troubled, sad, and finally rather foolish. The Republic provoked his alarm and disapproval; the war brought estrangement from his brother, causing both of them pain, and finally news of Antonio's death. The new Spain, deprived of most of its best writers, tried to restore him to the status of an important poet when he had long ceased to be one. Manuel Machado's best work is part of the finest flowering of Spanish *modernismo*, and so belongs to the first decade of the century, for by the end of that decade *modernismo* had been decisively transformed into other things by greater poets than Machado, among them his brother Antonio.

For many Spaniards today, Antonio Machado (1875-1939) stands in much the same relation to his contemporaries as does Baroja. The literary achievements and importance of poets such as Darío and Jiménez, like those of Valle-Inclán and Pérez de Ayala, are respectfully acknowledged, but Antonio Machado is the poet of his generation whose work is actually read in Spain. As in Baroja's case, the reasons are partly a matter of current literary taste, and partly ideological. For a great many readers, Machado is pre-eminently the author of certain poems in the second half of *Campos de Castilla*, which express most directly his ideas about what is wrong with Spain. Yet they are neither his most typical nor his best poems. Educated in the Institución Libre de Enseñanza, and brought up in the earnestly progressive atmosphere of a family whose head was a university teacher and a positivist, Machado seems to have felt the need, when he left home, for a rest from moral seriousness and social concern. His early adult life in Madrid and Paris was as bohemian as his brother's, and his first book of poems, *Soledades* (1903; augmented and revised as *Soledades, galerías y otros poemas*, 1907), belongs unequivocally to the Spanish *modernista* movement.

Again it is necessary to stress the word Spanish, for there are no fauns, princesses, or swans in *Soledades*, and as Machado himself said in a prologue to the 1917 edition of the book, although he admired Darío, 'el maestro incomparable de la forma y la sensación', he wanted from the start to take a different path, 'mirando hacia dentro'. *Soledades* does this, and constitutes a deep meditation on a theme of time and memory. Most of the poems were written when Machado was in his twenties, but their tone is that of a sad, weary old man whose soul is empty of the poetry that once delighted it: poetry, not in the sense of written verse, but as a long-lost experience of beauty and happiness, carried away for ever by the relentless flow of time. This flow, ending inexorably in death, was as much Machado's lifelong preoccupation as it was Unamuno's. The first poem of *Soledades* introduces 'el tictac del reloj' which was to resound through all Machado's verses: a hateful sound, for present

time is always bitter and barren. This is the starting-point of his poetic
meditation, and the beautiful poems of this first book of verse are
punctuated by a recurrent series of harsh words—'hastío', 'monotonía',
'bostezo', 'amargura', 'llorar'—whose message is summed up in the
uncompromising lines:

Ya nuestra vida es tiempo, y nuestra sola cuita
son las desesperantes posturas que tomamos
para aguardar . . . Mas Ella no faltará a la cita.   (xxxv)[2]

And yet, he recalls in other poems, there was a time when it
seemed that there was more to life than choosing a posture in which
to wait for death. Joy once passed by the poet's door. It may not pass
again, but its memory remains, like the fragrance of dead roses, in the
joyless present. Memory, however, can mean different things, as
Henri Bergson said, in terms which Machado, when he attended the
French philosopher's lectures in 1910, was to recognise as an exposition of his own intuitions. To remember that there was a time of
happiness does not in itself make one happy, rather the reverse. But
there is a way, elusive and uncertain, of reliving the emotions of past
experience, and to this way Machado applies, in a special sense, the
word 'soñar'. As Bergson was to observe, the custom of separating
past from present time has a useful logical neatness, but it bears little
relation to the reality of consciousness, where the past always endures
in some way in the present. Machado's *sueños* make this duration a
central function and subject of poetry; they are ways of escaping from
'el tictac del reloj' into a world spun from the webs of memory. 'De
toda la memoria, sólo vale/el don preclaro de evocar los sueños'
(LXXXIX) is his most clear and concise statement of the idea. But
deliberate evocation of the past in waking life is difficult, and
Machado's *Soledades* pursues the shadows of dreams in moods which
vary from hope to despair. His poems characteristically take the form
of a dialogue, with the seasons, the dawn, the night, asking questions
to which there is often no answer.

Though he persists in seeking the consolation of the dream which
permeates the grey present with luminous memory, it is the act of
seeking, rather than the recovered dream, which forms the subject of
Soledades. For this reason the poems mysteriously cross and recross
the frontiers between dream and reality, past and present. Often they
start from the contemplation of a real present scene, or from a
moment in the past into which Machado then tries to bring the

memory of a more remote past. They also describe real things, but the objects described then evoke other things from the world of dreams, and so take on much more than a descriptive value. Sometimes, as in a line like 'Donde acaba el pobre río la inmensa mar nos espera' (XIII), or in a poem like 'La noria' (XLVI), the symbolism is of a simple kind where it is possible to speak of what each image stands for in reality. But *Soledades* also reveals the special importance to Machado of a small number of images which he repeats again and again, and which clearly have no single or simple 'meaning', but are used for their multiple evocative power and as a source of different meditations. The image of the garden, for example, certainly sometimes recalls the actual garden of Machado's infancy in Seville,[3] and so suggests a theme of the lost paradise of childhood. In the retrospective 'Retrato' which introduces *Campos de Castilla*, Machado describes it factually as 'un huerto claro, donde madura el limonero' (XCVII). But many of the gardens of his poems are very different. In a later poem of different tone, the same real garden with its lemon tree becomes 'un huerto sombrío' (CXXV), and in *Soledades* the garden, as well as being a 'jardín encantado del ayer', is also sometimes a dark, damp, sad place. When he is in a mood of despair, the imagined garden (usually not 'huerto' now, but 'jardín' or 'parque') is less the sunlit memory of infancy than the melancholy, abandoned, aristocratic park of Verlaine, Valle-Inclán, Jiménez, and the other *modernistas*, and exudes a very different kind of nostalgia. The same fertile variety of significance is contained in the image of the fountain, which in *Soledades* does many things. It sings the happy song of the poet's lost childhood, it sobs monotonously, echoing the boredom of present existence, it flows like life and time into the marble bowl of death, and it dries up like the poet's joy. Similarly the 'caminos' that wind through Machado's poems are sometimes the actual dusty roads that he so often walked, sometimes the roads of life leading to western horizons, sometimes those of his wanderings through the corridors of the soul, whose twists and turns he follows without knowing their destination. This last uncertainty is emphasised in his later poetry by his likening of the road of life to the wake of a ship, a neat existential image of life as merely the history of an individual's deeds. The evening light which so often illuminates the roads can also create a peaceful atmosphere which encourages memory to dream its dreams, but it can equally be the light of a 'tarde cenicienta y mustia' (LXXXVII), causing anguished reflections on decay and death.

In spite of the fine perceptions and moving evocations of this introspective poetry, Machado came to feel that it was not achieving anything. Perhaps he did not realise that it was expressing with great poignancy the sorrow of not achieving anything, and was fulfilling as few other poems in Spanish had done its stated aim: 'Mirar lo que está lejos/dentro del alma' (LXI). Whatever the case, his next and best-known book of poems, *Campos de Castilla* (1912; augmented in a second edition of 1917), deliberately turns outwards to look at landscape, people, history, and to reflect on the state of Spain and the eternal character of her people. This is the book that makes Machado 'the poet of the Generation of '98'. Although the change is celebrated by some readers as the moment when he emerged from his brooding uncertainty and found his true, strong voice, the loss was at least as great as the gain. *Campos de Castilla* contains some very fine poems, when Machado filters his impressions through his acute poetic sensibility; but he was a poet gifted above all with introspective perspicacity, and the change of direction produced shallower poetry, some of it downright banal.

The change of style was connected with important events in his personal life. In 1907 he gave up his bohemian ways for the obscure life of a schoolmaster in Soria, where, like the Basque Unamuno and the Valencian Azorín, the Andalusian Machado experienced the powerful attraction of the austere, stony heartland of Spain. After two years in the ancient, quiet town on its high, bleak plateau, Machado, now thirty-four, married a girl of sixteen. For a brief while Leonor filled his great inner loneliness with deep and tender love. But in 1911, while they were visiting Paris, Machado's young wife gave the first signs that she was dying from tuberculosis. He nursed her desperately for a year in Soria, but she died in August 1912. After her death he moved to another quiet provincial capital, Baeza, in the northern reaches of his native Andalusia, where he continued to write poems which were incorporated in the 1917 edition of *Campos de Castilla,* but which for the most part are only tenuously connected with the theme of the book's title.

In the early poems of the collection, Machado's basic material is description of real landscape, the harsh Castilian highlands which are matched so well to his direct, sinewy style, where a handful of images and phrases fulfil his purposes well enough for him not to bother to find alternatives, but simply to repeat them. The descriptions, however, turn readily into meditations, and the main themes of

Soledades are still present, though in a changed form. For Machado is now observing as a national phenomenon what had formerly been a matter of personal anguish: the grey monotony and barrenness of the present with its intimations of a vanished glory in the past. There was a time, in the infancy of Castile, when Soria stood on its advancing frontiers, tense and strong, like a loaded crossbow at the head of a nation of indomitable warriors spurred on by high ideals. Now all is ruin and decay; the race of heroes has degenerated into a sullen peasantry whom Machado invariably describes (in spite of the acclaim he has won as a poet of the people) as an ugly, vicious, graceless population of 'atónitos palurdos sin danzas ni canciones', governed by primitive superstition and base instinct.

Much of this descriptive poetry, with its concise flashes of memory of the greatness of Castile, is powerful and convincing, and has a rugged beauty that would make Machado a major poet even if he had never written anything else. There are other excellent things in *Campos de Castilla,* like the seven tender, tragic poems written (in Baeza) on the subject of Leonor's death, or the long narrative poem 'La tierra de Alvargonzález'. The latter is a rather unusual work, a modern *romance* which resumes many of the themes of *Campos de Castilla* and attempts to project a reformist's vision of the ills of modern Spain through a legendary treatment of elemental human wickedness. Unamuno admired the poem greatly. But at times it comes very close to the failings of the weaker poems of the rest of the volume, which are the ones where Machado speaks plainly about his view of Spain's social and political problems. His view was basically the admirable and honourable one he had learnt in the Institución Libre de Enseñanza, but it did not often make for good poetry. 'Llanto de las virtudes y coplas por la muerte de don Guido' is acceptable as a minor exercise in irony, and 'Del pasado efímero', 'Los olivos', and 'El mañana efímero' have some memorable lines; but their pretensions to define a national malady do not bear close examination, and their intellectual content is nebulous and sometimes emptily rhetorical. The sudden appearance in some of these poems of 'buenos aldeanos' and 'benditos labradores' looks like a lapse into sentimental wishful thinking. At any rate, we are given no clue as to how to distinguish them from the degenerate, bushy-browed 'palurdos' of the other kind.

After Leonor's death, Machado confessed to a drying-up of his poetic powers—'Se ha dormido la voz en mi garganta' (CXLI). In a poem written soon after his return to Andalusia he noted sadly that his recollections of childhood lacked the element of dream—'mas falta el hilo que el recuerdo anuda/al corazón' (CXXV)—although in 'A José María Palacio' (CXXVI), dated by Machado less than a month later than the previous poem, the 'don preclaro' seems to be working again in his moving reminiscences of Castile and Leonor. To the end of his days he remained capable of writing very fine poems with all the power and beauty of his earlier poetic voice. But he rarely did so. In Baeza he began to devote more of his time to philosophical study, and to expressing his own philosophical reflections in aphorisms like those of the 'Proverbios y cantares' of *Campos de Castilla* (CXXXVI) and *Nuevas canciones* (CLXI). It was also at this time that he invented his two 'apocryphal professors', Abel Martín and Juan de Mairena. Machado's compilations of their poems, sayings, extracts from lectures and classes, accompanied by his own comments, allowed him to continue his lifelong dialogue with himself, and to present ideas of his own in a framework of self-effacing irony. Many of these bits and pieces, especially those collected in *Juan de Mairena*, consider poetry itself, and together with Machado's poetic aphorisms constitute an important store of his ideas about poetry. A number of them expound his dislike of baroque ornamentation in poetry, and of the 'Gongorism' and cult of metaphor for its own sake, which he observed as characteristic of the rising generation of Spanish poets. But his most interesting remarks are the ones he makes about the relation of time to poetry and the difference between poetry and logic. These remarks are scattered through his later writing, but resumed most concisely and thoughtfully in the 'Poética' he supplied for Gerardo Diego's anthology *Poesía española* in 1931. Machado's remarks deserve careful attention, but their basic point is that modern poetry, unlike logic, has to try to extract what is eternally true from what is constantly changing, and that the way to do this is to recognise that the essence of life is, paradoxically, its temporality. He concludes:

> El poeta profesa, más o menos conscientemente, una metafísica existencialista, en la cual el tiempo alcanza un valor absoluto. Inquietud, angustia, temores, resignación, esperanza, impaciencia que el poeta canta, son signos del tiempo, y al par, revelaciones del ser en la conciencia humana.

This is both a penetrating general observation and an illuminating statement of Machado's own poetic aims. The curious fact is, however, that from 1917 onwards, his own poetry responds less and less to his theories, and his philosophical poetry is mostly abstract and intellectual.[4] The one great exception is 'Poema de un día' (CXXVIII), which combines all that is best in Machado in a philosophic meditation that flows directly out of an acute sense of the passing of time in the real, monotonous atmosphere of Baeza on a rainy day.

In 1917 Machado moved to Segovia, where his outward life became busier. He became involved in the university extension movement, and spent much of his time in Madrid. From 1926 onwards he wrote many plays in collaboration with his brother Manuel. An autumnal, but apparently very happy, love-affair inspired the group of poems called 'Canciones a Guiomar'. When the Republic came, he devoted himself to its cultural and educational projects, and throughout the war he remained in Spain, writing and lecturing in the service of the Republican cause as far as his failing health would allow. The final advance of the Nationalist armies forced him at last to leave Spain, crossing the Pyrenees with his aged mother one bitter January night in 1939 to the small French port of Collioure. He died a month later, and was buried in Collioure, where his remains still lie.

At first sight, no poet could be further removed from Machado than Juan Ramón Jiménez (1881-1958), the pale aesthete and sickly recluse who spent most of his life apparently fleeing from the world's problems into the private obsessions of his art, his hypochondria, his morbid fear of death, and a whole catalogue of lesser manias. Yet Machado and Jiménez have more in common than is often allowed, particularly in their early work. Jiménez was by no means a total recluse. Summoned to Madrid in 1900 by Darío and Villaespesa to support the battle for *modernismo*, he made the indispensable visit to Paris, where he became directly acquainted with the work of Verlaine, Mallarmé, and the Symbolists. For five years, even though his poor health forced him to retire for long periods to a sanatorium in the Guadarrama, he played a busy part in the literary life of Madrid. In 1905 he returned to his home town of Moguer in order to devote himself more completely to writing and reading for the next seven years, but he maintained abundant contact with the outside world, and kept a watchful eye on what was happening to poetry, inside and outside Spain.

Nevertheless it is true that no poet has dedicated himself so totally to his art as Juan Ramón Jiménez. For him, poetry was a means of seeking personal salvation, a fact which makes his work difficult, and, to some readers, irritating in its complete and sometimes hermetic self-absorption. Although his lifelong practice of revising, suppressing, and selectively rearranging his immense poetic production shows that he was minutely concerned with how his work should be read, in the end communication is a secondary matter for Jiménez. In the 'Poética' he submitted to the first (1932) edition of Diego's anthology he said: 'Yo tengo escondida en mi casa, por su gusto y el mío, a la Poesía. Y nuestra relación es la de los apasionados'. In the second (1934), augmented edition he refused to have any of his poems published at all. The rich rewards to be had from reading Jiménez's poems are, in a sense, merely the by-products of his passionate relationship with poetry. The reader may well feel that he is only an eavesdropper on Jiménez's narcissistic, ecstatic experience, and is unable to identify himself with its central purpose. He may even feel that its central purpose is a kind of madness.

The adolescent sentimentality of Jiménez's first two books of poems, *Ninfeas* and *Almas de violeta* (1900), caused him to repudiate them in later life. After these books, his whole, vast poetic output throughout half a century is a single, untiring quest of some kind of Absolute through poetry, through the struggle to find the appropriate language and concepts for his experience. The poems of what has come to be regarded as his 'first period'—from *Rimas* (1902) to *Sonetos espirituales* (1914-15)—characteristically look at creation and fail to perceive its meaning, or the individual's relation to it. But at the same time Jiménez is agonisingly aware of his intense longing to apprehend something that lies behind the surface of things, without knowing what that something might be. 'Qué triste es amarlo todo,/ sin saber lo que se ama' (*TA* 12).[5] What perplexes and pains him most at this period is the transience of all life, and in this he resembles Machado closely. Many poems meditate on the subject of his own death, but normally not in any morbid or private way. Poems like 'El viaje definitivo (*TA* 123), which begins: '...Y yo me iré. Y se quedarán los pájaros/cantando;' capture with elegant simplicity a cruel enigma with which most people are familiar. Few poets have made such beautiful poetry as Jiménez out of the sadness of seeing living things as things which will die, or the sorrow of the loveliness of hopeful beginnings—spring, dawn, budding flowers—which will end so soon. The symbols with which he explores the mystery of time and essence are conventional enough, but Jiménez invests them with

personal implications. Though he uses as symbols of life and hope all
the aspects of natural life which readily lend themselves to such association, his attitude to these signs is one of frustration and at times
hatred, because the hope is false. A life symbol, for Jiménez, is pre-
eminently a symbol of what will eventually die. So he turns away
from them to their opposites, searching among symbols of death and
decay for something truer, nearer to the eternal, absolute essence that
is his goal.

There is little in this poetry that is esoteric or beyond the realm
of ordinary experience. Poems like the one beginning

> Tú acompañas mi llanto, marzo triste,
> con tu agua.
> — Jardín, ¡cómo tus rosas nuevas
> se pudren ya en el fondo de mi alma! — ...   (TA 254)

play neatly with immediately intelligible images to express a sensitive,
melancholy man's anguish at the cruel way in which time wipes out
every promise of joy provided by life. Nor is it difficult to respond
to his intuitions about how a state of decay or death—winter, the
setting sun, night-time, moonlight—is more impervious to the passing
of time, and therefore more consoling, than a state of birth or early
growth. But Jiménez goes rather further than this in his search for
eternal essence within temporality. He once claimed that he always
had been and always would be a Platonist,[6] and there comes a point
when readers who have not been and will not be Platonists must
begin to part company with him. That is to say that Jiménez was
anxious to believe that behind the appearance of things there is an
absolute and eternal essence which exists independently of human
consciousness, and that the Poet may be privileged with intuitions of
this essence and its 'immanence' in the accidents of experience. A
recent study of Jiménez's poetry argues that Jiménez subscribed to
the belief that 'the psychic content of any verbal artifact is eternal
and independent of the fate of the artifact as an empirical entity',[7]
and that the act of naming elements of his experience (the psychic
content of his poems, that is) would transcend and survive the
physical existence of his books of verse. The response of non-
Platonists to such a concept is bound to be that it is mistaken, and
that Jiménez, like Plato, was deeply misguided, but in a way that was
rich in incidental perceptions. The Platonic longings of a poem like
'La espiga' (TA 122), which speaks of an

anhelo inestinguible
ante la norma única de la espiga perfecta,
de una suprema forma, que eleve a lo imposible
el alma, ¡oh poesía! infinita, áurea, recta!

may command respect as longings for the impossible, but when they turn into affirmations they begin to tread a mystic path where few can follow.

But, amazingly, the path trod by Jiménez led him to his goal. Until 1916, for all his intimations of immortality, his poetry conveys a message of frustration and despair. In 1916 he crossed the Atlantic and married Zenobia Camprubí Aymar in the United States. Both experiences were to be of fundamental importance to his poetry. His wife was a woman of wide culture, a talented translator of poetry (notably that of Rabindranath Tagore), who helped him a great deal in his literary work. She also performed the exacting task of putting up with him, nursing him and running his practical affairs so that he could isolate himself from the world and bury himself in 'la Obra', as he invariably described his work. But the trip to America and back also provoked a crisis in his poetry. He found the experience of being on the open sea for days deeply disturbing, and in his striving to express to himself the enigma of the ocean's uniqueness, his poetry and his quest took an important step forwards. The experience is related, in a way that cannot be summarised, in the poems and prose of *Diario de un poeta reciencasado* (1916), whose title Jiménez changed in 1948 to *Diario de poeta y mar* for the express purpose of emphasising the importance of his experience of the sea. It was a remarkable experience: only a man so dedicated to the belief that poetry is a path to ultimate truth could have evolved a new conception of the significance of his own life out of a struggle with words. For during the journey, Jiménez began to glimpse the possibility that the divine enchantment he sought, which had made him weep with longing for he knew not what, might reside within himself. The vision of the Absolute within his grasp alternately elates him and provokes cautiously ironic commentaries on his own elation. But in two 'Nocturnos' written on the voyage home, he speaks of how his soul is about to take possession of an 'imperio infinito' (*TA* 328) and a 'dominio eterno' (*TA* 329).

His next book of poems was boldly entitled *Eternidades* (1916-17), and opens with a series of statements—similar to those made by W. B. Yeats two years earlier, almost certainly known to Jiménez—announcing his dissatisfaction with all his previous poetry, which he regarded as overdressed, smothered under an excessive load of imagery. From now on, he says, intelligence is to be his muse, and his poetic task, to capture 'el nombre exacto de las cosas' (*TA* 339). Intelligence and exactness had not been absent from his earlier work; he had always been concerned with meaning. But he had often tried to convey it vaguely and impressionistically, as Verlaine had required. Now his poems become much more conceptual, and much more difficult. It is necessary to approach each of them as a complex and subtle mental problem which will render up its full meaning after only patient reflection. Although the same could be said of much good poetry, it is usually possible to get something from a quick first reading of a poem, whereas in Jiménez's later poetry this kind of reading communicates absolutely nothing.

This 'poesía desnuda', as he called it, freer in form and more epigrammatic than his earlier verse—as if he were now afraid that metrical patterns, rhyme and assonance, might distract attention from the poem's impact on the intellect—follows an astonishing mystical path upwards towards final ecstasy, growing ever more confident in successive triumphs of self-discovery. A major triumph was that of coming to terms, at least in his poetry, with death. As is often the case with Jiménez's poetry, his poems on death invite the reader to consider different levels of interpretation. At a deep metaphysical level, his apprehension of the significance of death will seem to many readers profoundly silly. Jiménez realised that one way of achieving the mystic's characteristic desire to annihilate individual consciousness by merging it in a greater totality is simply to die, and he made a great deal of this idea in his poetry. But as always, his keen intelligence and insights succeed in bringing this bizarre idea to bear on more ordinary human experience, for he was also clearly alert to the much more immediate sense in which death gives meaning to life. If we never died, most of what we mean when we talk of life would lose its significance, even its value. This is the concept with which he makes brilliant play in a poem like '¿Cómo, muerte, tenerte miedo?' (*TA* 469), neatly turning the traditional idea of death on its head. His death only has existential significance while he is still alive. When he dies, that will be the death of his death, so . . .

> . . . ¿No seré yo,
> muerte, tu muerte, a quien tú, muerte,
> debes temer, mimar, amar?

Thus the symbolic paradoxes which run through the whole of his poetry, which started as anguished queries, are beginning to change into exultant affirmations of a Platonic kind. Their common theme is that in the ideal world behind the 'real' one, the apparent qualities of many things are turned into their opposites. His old feeling, for instance, that spring was a symbol of dying whereas autumn affirmed something closer to the ideal (*TA* 275) develops into the full-blown definition of autumn as 'inmortal primavera' (*TA* 387). One of his many poems entitled 'La muerte' (*TA* 539) similarly opens by describing death as 'Vida, divina vida', a consummation devoutly to be wished. The difference between Jiménez and more orthodox Platonic or religious mystics is that he does not seek to cut himself off from the physical, transient world. Indeed he revels in his growing perception of how the transcendental world of the ideal gives meaning and joy to the material world. The succession of nature's seasons is no longer sad because beneath it exists 'la estación total'. The road of life will come to an end, but that does not matter, because beside it runs 'la corriente infinita', the river of eternity. The joy which Jiménez finds in this duality is not characteristic of most mystical experience. The original title of his last major book, *Animal de fondo* (1947), refers to himself, a creature of divine, eternal depths, but still a human animal. In 1949 the book was republished under the general title of its new second part, *Dios deseado y deseante*. The god is an unusual and mysterious one, though he may not seem so at first sight. In the Notes to *Animal de fondo* (*TA* pp. 1016-19) Jiménez describes himself as a pantheistic mystic, and speaks of 'un dios vivido por el hombre en forma de conciencia inmanente', so that it might seem natural to assume that the 'dios deseado y deseante' means his own divine inner longing finding the object of its desire in the outer world. But it is by no means as simple as that. In a poem like 'La forma que me queda' (*TA* 688) it is clear that the divinity he finds in nature is the 'dios deseante' and that the 'dios deseado' resides in his own soul. More commonly, however, the two are fused into a single, ineffable experience of ecstasy and certainty, the glorious culmination of a lifetime of poetic inquiry.

Or so it should have been. But Jiménez was unable to sustain his vision through the remaining years of his life. They were troubled years. Jiménez's health was failing, and he spent much time in hospital. Zenobia developed cancer, and though an operation gave them a few years of hope, she died in 1956, only a few days after

4 * *

Jiménez had been awarded a Nobel Prize. What little poetry he wrote in his last years is greatly subdued in tone, and hardly alludes at all to the wonderful experience recorded in *Dios deseado y deseante*. But Jiménez's relapse into melancholy and anxiety makes his previous rapture all the more remarkable. Like more orthodox mystics, he had evidently felt himself in a state of grace, vouchsafed, perhaps, as a reward for his long years of faith and devotion; also like other mystics, he found that the state was not an enduring one, and his last years were spent waiting, submissively and in vain, for it to return.

All the poetry considered so far reflects to some degree a series of assumptions which give it a certain unity, and which derive largely from French poetry and from Bécquer, who introduced into Spanish poetry the idea that the Poet's special gift is not one of expression, but of perception of the inexpressible, so that his special task and torment is to struggle with the inadequacies of language. Since the new poetry wished to react against the senseless ugliness and vulgarity of modern life, it was a foregone conclusion that it could not appeal to a wide audience. More than any before them, the poets of this period wrote for each other.

The poetry of Unamuno, as might be expected, adopts a characteristic posture of opposition to all such assumptions. Although he only began to publish poetry in 1907 with his volume *Poesías*, it is well to remember that he was three years older than Darío and seventeen years older than Jiménez. His formative reading in poetry had been, not Mallarmé and Verlaine, but Dante, Milton, Leopardi, Tennyson, and Carducci. Unamuno was opposed to musicality, sensuousness, and excessive imagery in poetry, and wrote harsh, rough-hewn verses which are often powerful and moving in exactly the same way as his prose writing. This makes his achievement as a poet difficult to assess. Cernuda thought him the best poet of his time, neglected purely because his poetry was unfashionable in both manner and matter.[8] That it was so is undeniable. In forthright, unpolished verses it deals with the subjects that concerned Unamuno most deeply—human relations, Spain, and man's longing for God and immortality. One of his major poetic ventures, in an age which preferred its poetry to be brief and pagan, was his long religious meditation, *El Cristo de Velázquez* (1920), inspired by the famous painting in the Prado.

But even Cernuda admits that he considers Unamuno a fine poet in all his writings, that is to say, a poet in the sense that he was not a systematic, analytic thinker, but preferred to express his intuitions and emotions in a spontaneous way. This is a legitimate view: it would be excessively pedantic to insist that the term poetic cannot be applied to *Del sentimiento trágico* or *San Manuel Bueno*. But in the more conventional sense of the word poetry, it must be admitted that Unamuno was dogmatically insensitive to the qualities of poetry that was different from his own. In his insistence that poetry was not like music, for instance, he understood music in the narrow sense of harmonious sounds, whereas other poets, particularly since Verlaine and the Symbolists, had paid attention to poetry's capacity for affecting the feelings directly as music does, and, as Schopenhauer had said, for speaking to something subtler than the intellect. Hence Verlaine's title, *Chansons sans paroles*, and, at one remove, Jiménez's definition of a poet as one who 'coge el encanto de cualquier cosa . . . y deja caer la cosa misma'. On the subject of imagery, Unamuno is similarly insensitive:

> ¿Imágenes? Estorban del lamento
> la desnudez profunda,
> ahogan en flores
> la solitaria nota honda y robusta . . .

Apart from the fact that these lines employ images themselves, the idea they express takes no account of the image's concise power to force the reader to make an association of concepts into an act of personal discovery. Moreover, if images are a distraction, metre and assonance ought to be too, yet Unamuno kept closely to formal poetic structures, and a great many of his best poems are sonnets.

What he will not recognise is that, since the natural form of verbal expression is prose, when a writer—at any rate in modern times—turns to poetry as we normally understand the word, it is because he wants to attempt something which he thinks prose cannot achieve. Unamuno does not conceive of poetry in these terms, and as a result, what is valuable in his poetry is exactly the same as what is valuable in his prose. His verse is often impressive in its intellectual force and its deep feeling, but it lacks poetic qualities. This is not to say that to be poetic, poetry now had to conform to the formulas of a Verlaine or a Jiménez—some of the poems of *Campos de Castilla* are sufficient proof of this—but that we have a right to expect modern poetry to provide, by implication, some kind of answer to the question of why the author did not say what he had to say in plain prose.

The extraordinary wealth of fine poetry produced in the twenties and thirties by the outstanding writers sometimes called the Generation of 1927 owes much to the poets mentioned so far. This generation, whose major figures include Guillén, Lorca, Alberti, Salinas, Cernuda, and Aleixandre (and whose work considered as a whole will inevitably carry us well beyond the end of the period being discussed in this section) never ceased to regard Unamuno, the Machados, Jiménez, and Darío and Bécquer before them, with respect, even when some of their seniors began to express disapproval for what the younger men were doing. But smooth continuity of development was inevitably jolted somewhat by the First World War and its political, social, and psychological consequences in both Spain and the rest of Europe. The arts responded to the traumatic experience of a horrible war, and the unsettling one of feeling that it had given birth to a new epoch, with a nervous outburst of levity. The first rumblings of an avalanche of '-isms' which fell on art had, in fact, been heard in Spain before the war. As early as 1909, Gómez de la Serna, always in the vanguard of everything, had introduced Spaniards to Marinetti's Futurism, with its iconoclastic call to break totally with the past, and its crazed exaltation of the machines, noise, speed, and violence of the twentieth century. But it was only in 1918 that the self-styled *ultraísta* group started its effort to keep Spain abreast of the tides of Cubism, Dadaism, Surrealism, and the like, which were running in Europe. The manifestos of *ultraísmo* merit little attention (and their direct results in poetry none at all), but they contributed something of importance to the best poetry of the period by asserting more vigorously than ever before the need to free poetry from reason and logic, by treating art as a wild game without rules, by their playful audacity in juxtaposing incongruous images and concepts, and in what they took from *creacionismo*. This *-ismo* made its way into Spain mainly through contact with the Chilean poet Vicente Huidobro (1893-1948), who lived in Paris, wrote part of his work in French, claimed to have invented *creacionismo,* and produced many atrocious examples of it. In reality it was not all that new. It is merely an extreme version of what is normally known as 'autonomous art'. The idea is that every last vestige of referential or representational purpose should be eliminated from art. Each work should be a new, independent entity, created, as Huidobro said, as nature creates a tree. When the art in question is poetry, images obviously acquire a central importance and a special function. They are no longer intended as metaphors of something else, they are not even Jiménez's 'encanto de cualquier cosa', but self-contained psychic experiences, like the experience of a phrase of music.

Better poets than Huidobro or the *ultraístas* drew what they felt was of use to their art from the wave of extravagant, self-advertising avant-garde theorising that followed the war. By doing so, they brought on their heads the grave disapproval of poets like Unamuno, Antonio Machado, and Jiménez, who regarded poetry as a deeply serious way of making sense of human experience and as having something to do with truth. The older poets were right in thinking that the motley artistic buffoonery of the Jazz Age and its host of tiny shooting stars was largely a transient lunacy; their own poetry now seems incomparably more modern than the antics of the *ultraístas*. But they were wrong in thinking that serious poetry had to follow their example exclusively and eschew all that the feverish fashions of the twenties offered. The younger poets took inspiration for their highly original and individual work from where it pleased them, from their immediate Spanish predecessors, from contemporary European experimental art, and from a wide selection of older Spanish writers. Their admiration for Góngora—the Góngora of the *Soledades*—and their commemoration of the tercentenary of his death are what earned them the title of the Generation of 1927. In the case of Góngora their aim was to call attention to great poetry which had been neglected since Menéndez y Pelayo had judged it unfavourably in the nineteenth century, but they were equally conscious and proud of being the heirs to a literature which included all the hallowed names, and which through the centuries had drawn more from folk-poetry and song than had other cultivated literatures. The *romance* in particular attracted the attention of many of them.

The most obvious example of this last fact is in the work of Federico García Lorca (1898-1936), the most famous figure, though not necessarily the best poet, of the generation. Much of his fame derives from legends, as Unamuno would have called them, which are more or less irrelevant to his poetry. Firstly, he was a truly magnetic personality; the memoirs of those who knew him invariably depict him at the centre of an admiring group. When he came from Granada to Madrid in 1919, he lived at the Residencia de Estudiantes, that remarkable offshoot of the Institución Libre whose importance as a centre of cultural communication cannot be overestimated, and there he evidently charmed one and all with his multiple talents. Then there is the political legend. Whether Lorca's murder in 1936 was a planned political act or one of private, local viciousness, and however slight his interest in politics had been, it brought Lorca world-wide fame as a great poet cut down in his prime by Fascist barbarism. Finally there is the legend of Lorca as a spontaneous, childlike poet, whose art springs like magic from intuitions which defy analysis; an export version of this legend makes him an inspired primitive, singing of the exotic myths and customs of his un-European Andalusian tribe.

The period 1920-24, when Lorca composed *Libro de poemas*, *Poema del cante jondo*, *Primeras canciones*, and *Canciones*, is when he comes nearest to this last legend, though it is not very near. Many of the poems in his first book are very similar to Machado's *Soledades*, and even use the same images to brood sadly on time and death. But as Lorca feels his way forwards towards his own style, their rather stilted melancholy gives way to a vigorous injection of popular inspiration and a playful audacity in the coining of metaphor. Both these characteristics of his art, however, need some qualification. Lorca was knowledgeable and unsentimental about Andalusian folklore. The *Poema del cante jondo* culls all that is most sombre from flamenco song. Even the most authentic, traditional 'cante hondo' has its lighter side, but Lorca chooses largely to ignore it. There is hardly a poem in the collection without some sad or sinister note. And the *Canciones*, which contain the simplest and most lighthearted poems Lorca ever wrote, are not very simple or lighthearted. Although they make use of traditional children's rhymes, and often ostensibly address themselves to children, and although they sometimes seem to delight in the nonsensical inconsequentiality of such rhymes, the *Canciones* soon reveal that Lorca's interest in the folklore of childhood, and in the kind of response children make to verse and song, is an adult and sophisticated one. A poem like his four-line 'Nocturno esquemático' is not uncharacteristic of the *Canciones*:

> Hinojo, serpiente y junco
> Aroma, rastro y penumbra.
> Aire, tierra y soledad.
>
> (La escala llega a la luna.)

Obviously it is far from his purpose to reproduce naïve songs of innocence. Themes of frustration, loss, and death throw dark shadows over the playfulness of the poems. A most unchildlike and unplayful sexual motif appears in many of them. Poems like 'Nocturno esquemático' are not for or about children, and critics who have tried to understand some of their more puzzling imagery have rightly turned to Freud, Jung, and Frazer as well as to Andalusian folklore.

All this applies equally, if not more, to Lorca's next book, *Romancero gitano* (1928; but written in 1924-27). To what extent Lorca knew what he was doing in his poetry is a matter of debate. His own statements about his poetry vary greatly in this respect. In his 'Poética' in Diego's anthology he says: 'Si es verdad que soy poeta por la gracia de Dios—o del demonio—, también lo soy por la gracia de la técnica y del esfuerzo, y de darme cuenta en absoluto de lo que es un poema'. In a letter to Jorge Guillén written while he was working on the *Romancero*, he is fairly explicit about his intentions: '. . . procuro armonizar lo *mitológico gitano* con lo puramente vulgar de los días presentes', and he says that he hopes that gypsies will understand his images.[9] On the other hand, in a lecture on the *Romancero* which he gave in 1926 but which has only recently been published, he warns of the impossibility of 'explaining the meaning' of some of his imagery, and makes the rather discouraging statement that in his 'Romance sonámbulo'—a poem which has probably been read and discussed more than any other by Lorca—'. . . nadie sabe lo que pasa, ni aun yo, porque el misterio poético es también misterio para el poeta que lo comunica, pero que muchas veces lo ignora'.[10]

Such a confession may serve to remind those who wish to treat Lodca's poetry seriously of two characteristic difficulties it presents. The first is that some of the more mysterious associations of words understand his images.[9] On the other hand, in a lecture on the that Lorca himself may not have realised this. The famous, recurrent 'buey de agua' image has been explained tirelessly by editors and commentators as well as by Lorca himself, but there are undoubtedly many other metaphors more puzzling than this one which have a simple, but generally unknown, origin in some detail of Andalusian life or of Lorca's personal experience. The second problem is that whereas Lorca's symbolism is sometimes of a universal kind, intelligible to everyone, it sometimes bears highly personal connotations. The opening verses of 'Romance del emplazado', for example, contain the lines:

. . . .
Sino que limpios y duros
escuderos desvelados,
mis ojos miran un norte
de metales y peñascos
donde mi cuerpo sin venas
consulta naipes helados.

The images of advancing asleep towards magnetic mountains, of a man who is dead already because he knows he is fated to die, are readily acceptable expressions of the gypsy's belief (real, or invented by Lorca, it does not matter) that once death has been ordained there is nothing to be done but prepare to lie down and die with dignity. On the other hand, the *romance* ends by describing Amargo's death in these terms:

Y la sábana impecable,
de duro acento romano,
daba equilibrio a la muerte
con las rectas du sus paños.

—lines which require elucidation in terms of Lorca's personal belief that centuries of Roman occupation had left a permanent mark on the Andalusian character, and had given the people a sense of the importance of making death a deliberately dignified and harmonious end to life.

But there are also many obviously important and thematic symbols in Lorca's poetry which are frankly difficult to decipher. The 'Romance sonámbulo' is full of them, and begins with one of the most problematical of all:

Verde que te quiero verde.
Verde viento. Verdes ramas.

It will not do to guess vaguely at what such symbols *might* mean, or what they usually mean in other literature and mythology.[11] Symbols like the moon, colours, horses, water, fishes, are intended to convey certain definite impressions, not necessarily precise or even always the same, but not arbitrary or fortuitous either. Only by trying to find out what they are can the rich resources of Lorca's poetic art be fully enjoyed.

It must be admitted, however, that the task becomes exceedingly difficult in much of the poetry Lorca wrote after this, and especially in *Poeta en Nueva York* (1940; written 1929-30). When Lorca visited America in 1929 he was horrified by the brutally alien nature of what he found in the New York of the depression, and by what he failed to find—any roots in nature, any unifying mythology or collective dream to make sense of the faceless, violent, shattered society he saw. The poems have been called surrealist. Lorca was certainly acquainted with surrealist theories by this time, but his poems only approach the theories in the sense that his spiritual turmoil and bewilderment are directly reflected in a bewildering turmoil of fantastic, tormented images of emptiness, coldness, and violence. When he seeks natural forces—in flowers, animals, the negroes of Harlem, seasonal changes— they are either trapped or engulfed in blood and slime, or wander like souls in agony through a desolation of sterile materials. Withdrawal to the New England countryside gave him some respite and compara- tive peace, but he used it to write of a more personal sense of despair. When he returned to New York he completed his book with further denunciations of the city's hateful civilisation, and then escaped thankfully to Cuba. However, it seems likely that Lorca's poetry would have changed at this time without the experience of his visit to America. It is known, from his letters and conversations with friends, that he went abroad because of a feeling of frustration with his life in Spain. After *Poeta en Nueva York* he wrote less poetry, devoting more of his attention to the theatre. But most of the poetry he did write is stamped with anguish and inner torment which are still expressed in difficult and often obscure images. The one great exception to this is his *Llanto por Ignacio Sánchez Mejías,* the deeply felt elegy he wrote when this cultured bullfighter, friend of many of the poets of Lorca's generation, died in the ring in 1934. The four parts of the poem carry out the traditional function of a formal act of mourning, purging initial emotions of shock and horror, first by ritualised lament, then by calm meditation on death and decay, and finally by a serenely philosophic funeral oration. The first part recalls confused impressions of the actual goring in the ring and death in the infirmary, and reflects a state of mind still too shocked to separate the tragic reality from such insignificant details as the obsessively repetitious 'a las cinco de la tarde'. The second part, 'La sangre derramada', is still close to the actual event, and is an outpouring of personal grief and of an urge to escape from the fact of Ignacio's death. But it also tries to apprehend the significance of the death in terms of the symbolic mythology of the *Romancero gitano*. Although the terms may sometimes be related to ancient and universal mythological beliefs, they derive more immediately from Lorca's view of Andalusian folk-culture. In his lecture 'Teoría y juego del duende',[12] what he has to say about death and bullfighting in Spanish art often illuminates the concepts and images of this part of the *Llanto*. The third part, 'Cuerpo presente', is Lorca's farewell to his friend, a sorrowful but steady recognition that death has definitively, if somewhat mysteriously, claimed 'Ignacio el bien nacido'. The final part, 'Alma ausente', reflects, in much the same way as Jiménez's 'Viaje definitivo', on how Ignacio's familiar circumstantial world will continue to exist without giving any sign that it is bereft of his presence. The poet's song, however, will preserve Ignacio's memory 'para luego', says Lorca. Time has certainly proved him right. Ignacio Sánchez Mejías has continued to live in innumerable imaginations because of Lorca's lament. Its sincere sorrow, its dense, beautiful imagery, and its measured dignity make it a magnificent achievement, not only as a great elegy, but as a demonstration of a fine poet's ability to respond to a personal grief by turning from his theatrical work and from the dark, private preoccupations of his late poetry to produce this last fine monument to his poetic gifts.

Although Lorca's *Libro de poemas* of 1921 was the first important book of verse to be published by the poets who are now commonly grouped into his generation, the generation's senior member in terms of age was Pedro Salinas (1892-1951). Like many of his fellow-poets of the period, Salinas was a university teacher, and produced some notable studies of Spanish literature, especially after he left Spain for good in 1939. His poetic work up to the Civil War is contained in the volumes *Presagios* (1923), *Seguro azar* (1929), *Fábula y signo* (1931), *La voz a ti debida* (1933), and *Razón de amor* (1936). He was past thirty when he published his first book of verse, but the frivolity of the twenties and the extravagances of *ultraísmo* find echoes in his early work. His second and third books, particularly, celebrate the excitement of a world of fast cars, cinemas, electric lights, telephones, radiators, typewriters, and express a sense of fun and verbal exuberance shared by most of his contemporaries in this age of brittle gaiety.

But, taken as a whole, Salinas's work before 1936 shows that these are mere trappings to a single, sustained poetic purpose and a

constant basic theme: the paradoxical way in which the apparent
clarity and solidity of external reality changes, in subjective experience of it, into a mysterious complex of fleeting, tenuous impressions
and intuitions which it is very difficult to name or express exactly.
The aim of his poetry is therefore to explore the relation between
outer and inner reality, and to exploit the hints and premonitions
provided by inner experience that there is more to the outer world
than meets the eye. Some readers have seen this exploration as a
quest of something like Platonic Ideas, and it has to be admitted that
Salinas himself has given vague encouragement to such a view by
defining poetry (in Diego's anthology) as 'una aventura hacia lo
absoluto', which makes him sound like another Jiménez. And indeed,
amid the playful fantasies of his early work, and particularly in
Presagios, there are poems which find him standing sad and puzzled,
like the young Jiménez, looking at real things and trying to penetrate
their enigma, feeling an 'eterna ambición de asir/lo inasidero'. In the
first poem of *Presagios* his thoughts travel up from the ground, on
which his feet are solidly planted, to his head, and so to

> 'la idea pura, y en la idea pura
> el mañana, la llave
> —mañana—de lo eterno'.

But his long inquiry into the relationship between inner and outer
reality belies these Platonic intimations, and turns out to be very
unlike Jiménez's. He remains fascinated by the external world, its
perfect explicability and existence-in-itself. In 'Vocación' he opens
his eyes and finds the world perfect in the clear light of day; then
he closes them, and finds doubt and confusion. The laconic note on
which the poem ends is one of melancholy resignation: 'Cerré los
ojos'. But he soon has them open again, marvelling at the certainty of
what they see. All through *Seguro azar* and *Fábula y signo* he moves
restlessly between the two worlds suggested by the paradoxical titles,
endlessly comparing them and puzzling over their incompatibility,
fascinated especially by the 'geometría sin angustia' of things that
can be counted and measured exactly, or things that stand still and
solid in time and space, like the Escorial, to which two of his most
suggestive poems are addressed.

Fortunately, he did not remain for ever in a state of impotent
perplexity. Already in *Fábula y signo* the juxtaposition of the two
worlds produces subtle insights into the nature of both of them, and

such insights become of great interest in *La voz a tí debida*, a book of poems about love. The poems are not hymns of joy or sorrow, but discoveries about what love is, in the details of its moods and moments. To say that Salinas is seeking to define the essence of love would be to give the matter too abstract an air, though this is ultimately what he is after. He starts from common human feelings in a real love-affair with a real and individual woman. He then attempts to examine and define details of his experience with all the sensitivity and precision of which he is capable. In a sense he therefore leaves the woman behind, outside himself, but there is no question, as some readers seem to suppose, either of his 'escaping' into some higher world of pure spirit, or of his treating the reality of his beloved, as Bécquer sometimes did, as a nuisance which obtrudes on his inner experience. Lines like 'Su gran obra de amor / era dejarme solo' need careful integration into their context if they are not to be misunderstood. These two lines in fact end, with tender irony, an anecdotal poem which tells how his beloved, thinking him asleep, had drawn the blinds and tiptoed away. He was awake, but could not call out to her, since it would have destroyed the work of her loving care. In these poems, Salinas never goes outside the actual experience of his real love, but only deeper into it; the ideal, conceptualised 'tú' into which the body and lips of the woman often seem to dissolve, far from being any kind of Eternal Feminine, is Salinas's attempt to deepen his comprehension of what it is that he loves in this woman.

La voz a tí debida is the peak of Salinas's poetic achievement. His next book, *Razón de amor,* the last to be published before the war and exile changed his world, is shot through with anguish about fleeting time and the transience of happiness. The eager queries of his earlier poems turn into melancholy and fruitless doubt and a mood of sad resignation. There is poetry to be made out of such things, of course, and sometimes Salinas's sharp intelligence distils the essence of sentiments and impressions as skilfully as it ever did. After leaving Spain he wrote *El contemplado* (1946), in which he tries to recover his optimism by turning outwards again and observing the sunlit reality of Caribbean beaches, but *Todo más claro* (1949) and *Confianza* (1954), in spite of their titles, are made up mostly of gloomy reflections on modern civilisation and the shadow of the Bomb. There are fine poems in all these books, and in the posthumously published collection *Volverse sombra y otros poemas* (1957), but Salinas often becomes surprisingly long-winded and diffuse in his old age. Moreover, a mood of gloomy apprehension and melancholy resignation is a poor stimulant to a poet whose strength lay in making subtle discoveries. His secure position as a fine poet will continue to rest on the poems he wrote before 1936.

With few exceptions, the poets of this generation began their careers in a mood of high enthusiasm and gay poetic revelry, which later disintegrated, abruptly in some cases, more gradually in others, into sombre preoccupation with the human condition. No doubt this was due less to maturity than to the universal fading-away of the frail euphoria generated by the termination of the war to end all wars. In some other countries, the onset of a new despair turned some men's thoughts once again towards God, but in Spain very few found any consolation in religion.

One poet who presents a partial exception to the pattern of festive frivolity collapsing into despair is Jorge Guillén, born in 1893, but slower than others to consolidate his youthful poetic work into an important volume of verse, which he did in *Cántico* (1928). The absence of dramatic spiritual or artistic crises in his development is emphasised by the fact that for more than twenty years he worked on what is essentially one book, for *Cántico* was revised and enlarged in successive editions of 1936, 1945, and 1950. Furthermore, while the poetry of all his contemporaries in the twenties reflected in some measure the idea that art was a way of poking outrageous fun at life, Guillén's joy in living was from the beginning soberly and deeply felt, and *Cántico*, for the most part, is an extraordinary hymn to the perfection of things as they are.

Guillén, like Salinas at his best, submits the data of everyday experience to the scrutiny of a clear, analytic intelligence in order to extract what for him is their pure and glorious significance. His poetic creed, expressed in a letter which serves as his 'Poética' in Diego's anthology, is 'poesía bastante pura, *ma non troppo*'. That is to say that his purpose, like that of Salinas and of Valéry, whom he knew, admired, and translated, is to refine the essence of experience and discard specific, anecdotal dross; but at the same time he never loses sight of the fact that poetry is not some ineffable spiritual state, but poems written on a page, and made out of the raw material of our common human experience.

The accusation of abstract, 'dehumanised' intellectualism levelled at Guillén has long become a ninepin which commentators set up for the sake of knocking down; it is almost forgotten who accused him and why. But the point is, or was, that this poet of exuberant human emotions, who sings of humble, familiar details of everyday life, does not describe either the details or his emotions, but filters his impressions through his intellect and converts them into precise concepts. These he presents in strictly disciplined poetic structures, classical Spanish forms for the most part, but manipulated with the confidence warranted by his complete mastery of technique. Guillén loved order, precision, and balance in all things, and the formal perfection of his poems extends to the measured equilibrium of the total structure of each edition of *Cántico*. Since what he chiefly wishes to communicate is the wonder and delight afforded by ordinary things, sense impressions, though present in his poems, are but a springboard which projects him rapidly into an ecstatic fusion of emotion and intellect. 'Beato sillón' is not about an armchair, but about a beatific and certain contentment with life; and in a long, dense poem like 'Sol en la boda', although there are allusions to an actual wedding—fragrant flowers, candles, music, a crowd under the chestnut tree in the street outside the church—and even a faint thread of narrative as the ceremony proceeds, such allusions are so swift as to be hardly noticeable, merely a background to Guillén's extraordinary effort to wrest from this wedding the total significance of all such new beginnings.

The most superficial perusal of any few poems from *Cántico* reveals the book's central message, if only because Guillén repeats it so often and with such relish. It is the 'fábula', 'prodigio', 'maravilla' of the normal given world, to which he responds with rapture and amazement, though in what he regards as a perfectly normal way. The marvels are 'maravillas concretas', 'prodigios no mágicos'. He is not in a trance, nor does he perceive in reality any other-worldly significance hidden from lesser mortals. He is simply able to savour more often, and sustain for longer than most people can, the elated gladness, which everyone has known at some time, of being alive in a well-made world. Guillén's clear, ordered intellect often finds it appropriate to express this sense of perfection in geometrical terms, clean contours, symmetry of lines. Like Jiménez, he enjoys seeing the falling leaves of autumn reveal the skeleton of the bare trees. But his joy could not be more different from Jiménez's celebration of a deathly approximation to a mysterious ideal. Guillén also loved the buds of spring and the luxuriance of summer. In autumn he takes pleasure in the increased precision with which the bare branches define themselves, and accepts it as a further testimony of the sure, clear beauty of the created world. A further, revealing comparison with Jiménez is invited by Guillén's frequent use of images of ideal roundness. Both poets use the circle and the sphere as expressions of plenitude, but whereas Jiménez's circles are mystical Neoplatonic symbols of divinity, whose centre is everywhere and whose circumference is nowhere, as tradition has it, Guillén's 'perfección del círculo is a much less obscure expression of a sense of fullness, of standing under a noonday sun at the centre of an orb of perfection reaching to every horizon.

The author of *Cántico* was undoubtedly a lucky man, blessed with a serene and sunny disposition, and his book is a hymn of gratitude for the marvel of creation. The predominant outlook of *Cántico* can even be disturbing for some readers, who reasonably ask if we can really respect a mature man who has contrived to keep such a naïve optimism intact in twentieth-century Spain and Europe. The outlook itself does not, of course, produce fine poetry; if there were no more to Guillén than this, his work would not rise above the level of maddening popular songs which urge us to look on the bright side and count our blessings. So it comes as some relief to be able to observe that Guillén recognises the existence of ugliness, confusion, suffering, and death. In *Cántico* this recognition appears infrequently, and serves mainly to enhance, by contrast, Guillén's joy in being able to come out into the sunlight once again; but at least it gives a kind of guarantee of the authenticity of his joy, and makes it a little more accessible to less buoyant sensibilities. Guillén is not, after all, the bearer of a single, clear message. It is often very difficult to grasp what he wants to communicate, though the difficulty cannot be attributed to obscurity, but rather to an excessively piercing clarity. His poems demand an intellectual effort at least as great as the one that gave poetic form to his ideas and feelings. In the letter which Diego published as his 'Poética', Guillén explains that by pure poetry he understands simply what is left in a poem after all that is not poetry has been expunged. If the idea seems facile when put so barely, a careful look at any of his poems, particularly his longer ones, shows something of what he means. The purity is fundamentally a matter of conciseness, of omitting all the explanations necessary to prose. Sometimes Guillén compresses his concepts in so dense a poetic capsule that its explosive force is too great for the reader's mind; here lies the difficulty, and also the ultimate difference between poetry and prose. To take a very mild explosion from 'Sol en la boda' as an example, Guillén says of these two young people who have come to the altar: 'Nuevamente aquí están con su aventura / los dos eternos siempre juveniles'. Hardly any of the words would have the same meaning in a prose passage (the couple have not been married before, etc.); Guillén is leaping from the specific event towards a series of poetic insights into the meaning of anyone's wedding in anyone's total existence. Three lines later he reminds us, with superb economy, that their destiny will lead them to a 'final profundidad marina', three ordinary words which when put together in this context not only constitute a beautifully calm image of sinking into death, but crowd the mind with echoes of other literary voices as varied as those of Valéry, Machado, and Jorge Manrique.

With *Cántico* complete in its 1950 edition, Guillén began to build another great poetic edifice, *Clamor,* made up of *Maremagnum* (1957), *Que van a dar a la mar* (1960), and *A la altura de las circunstancias* (1963). The titles already suggest the change of tone which in the poems comes as a shock to the reader of *Cántico*. At long last Guillén seems to have broken under the weight of anguish that affected most of his contemporaries, to have stopped singing and emitted a great cry of pain and revulsion at the ugliness, cruelty, and confusion of a satanic world. Moreover, it is the concrete contemporary world of civil and world war, hurtling towards nuclear suicide, a world in which Guillén is growing old and feeling increasingly lost and helpless. Yet, as he himself has said, *Clamor* is not a negation of *Cántico*. The 'altura de las circunstancias', both personal and epochal, has tipped the balance. The suffering and insecurity which always stood threateningly at the edge of his joyous vision have broken loose and engulfed his joy. But this only means that it has become vastly more difficult to experience elation and hope, not that it has become impossible, and the tormented clamour, which seems at times to produce real obscurity in Guillén's poetry, gives way to moments of lucidity and serenity now and then.

In a third substantial volume, *Homenaje* (1967), which Guillén has said is to be his last, he finds a position somewhere between *Cántico* and *Clamor,* more concrete and accessible than in the former, less anguished and bitter than in the latter. He draws much consolation from art. Many of the poems are actual tributes to other poets, ancient and modern, Spanish and foreign. In these Guillén channels a lifetime's reading, and keen critical reflection on what he has read, into subtle poetic affirmations of the continuity of poetry as one great living tradition, and of the precious power of art to salvage treasures from the wreck of time. Guillén is still writing, but the imposing monument he has built out of *Cántico, Clamor,* and *Homenaje*—to which he has given the general title of *Aire nuestro*— needs no addition or embellishment to stand as one of the foremost poetic achievements of our time, totally realising the aim expressed in the 'Dedicatoria final' of the last edition of *Cántico*: Guillén addresses himself to 'ese lector posible que será amigo nuestro: ávido de compartir la vida como fuente, de consumar la plenitud del ser en la fiel plenitude de las palabras'.

Another member of the generation who is still writing poetry is Vicente Aleixandre (1898-), though unlike Guillén who has lived abroad and whose contact with Spain has been slight during the last thirty years, Aleixandre returned to Spain soon after the Civil War to become an important figure in the literary life of the nation and to exercise considerable influence on younger Spanish poets. His first book, *Ámbito* (1928), resembles Guillén's *Cántico* of the same year in its exultant celebration of the joy of being alive, but in little else. Its wild cries of pleasure in sensual delight, naked flesh and nights of passion, lack the intellectual and aesthetic discipline of Guillén's deeper rapture. The same lack of control detracts from Aleixandre's next two books, *Pasión en la tierra* (1935; written 1928-29), a collection of largely incomprehensible prose-poems, whose private subconscious ramblings Aleixandre tried to excuse later by calling them Freudian, and *Espadas como labios* (1932), which also insists on the supreme importance of mental and poetic freedom. No doubt such freedom is a fine and necessary thing in its proper place, but Aleixandre seemed to believe at this time that it was the be-all and end-all of poetry. His untiring enthusiasm for bringing puzzlingly incongruous concepts together, usually linking them simply with a blankly and rather insolently unhelpful 'o', or 'como' (as in 'Espadas como labios'), or 'hecho de', is very much a hit and miss affair. It may touch a responsive nerve in the reader's sensibility, but it will also cause some readers to recall with approval Guillén's remark in one of his lectures at Harvard in 1958—'There is no babble quite so empty as that of the subconscious left to its triviality'. The young Aleixandre was full of confidence in having achieved insights, and rarely seems to ask himself if they will also be insights for the reader.

Aleixandre's next three books, however, *La destrucción o el amor* (1935), *Mundo a solas* (1950; but written before the Civil War), and *Sombra del paraíso* (1944), have the maturity and control which were needed to turn his vivid poetic imagination to the production of interesting poetry. All three books were conceived as unities, and their poems make much more sense in the context of the whole book than if they are read separately. Their themes are mythical, in the primary sense that they offer poetic, non-rational accounts of why the universe is as it is. *La destrucción o el amor* speaks of an elemental natural force which unites all living things, and here the 'o' of the title is not gratuitous. In his own way Aleixandre is observing, as psychoanalysts and laymen have done before and since, the real relation between love and destructive violence, and expressing it in vivid images which challenge, but this time also reward, the imagination. The jungle ruled by this elemental force is real up to a point, for Aleixandre is considering its actual revelation in beasts of prey and their victims. But the jungle and its inhabitants also take their symbolic places in a mythological cosmogony, and are bounded on one side by the cold, black depths of a loveless, lifeless ocean, and on the other by an azure heaven to which the denizens of the forest reach up in hope, as they shrink from the dead sea. Without being an allegory of human life, the book is rich in compellingly allusive images of the human condition. The other two books relate more specifically to man's place in the cosmos. Their main myth, more human but less potently expressed in both books than in *La destrucción o el amor*, is that of paradise lost, and they present a bleak vision of human desolation and despair in a worn-out, corrupt, ephemeral world, where only the searching eye of the poet can perceive the last faint relics of the marvellous dawn of creation.

The ancient longing to escape from a hostile world back into a primeval innocence and security—of Eden, of childhood, of the womb—revived strongly in the twentieth century, in reaction to the previous century's predominant notion that the Golden Age lay in the future. In these books Aleixandre gives imaginative form to the dream and the despair that causes it. But it was his last foray either into myth-making or into the subconscious. His next important work, and the last of any consequence, *Historia del corazón* (1954), applies itself, as the poetry of post-war Spain was inclined to do, to the ordinary life of mankind. Aleixandre's poetic imagination, which once soared so daringly that it constantly risked tumbling dreadfully into obscurity, now flies very close to the ground. He writes simply of simple things, children, dogs, old age; though he writes thoughtfully, with sentiment and only occasional sentimentality, this is hardly the kind of thing Aleixandre's gifts fit him for. Since 1954 he has continued to write, but, unlike Guillén's, his work would surely have attracted little attention if it had not been signed by a famous name.

The most dramatic example of the personal and artistic trajectory traced by most of the poets of this generation is that of Rafael Alberti (1902-   ). Born and brought up in the Puerto de Santa María, on Andalusia's Atlantic coast, he was gifted, like Lorca, with a seemingly effortless ability to make poetry out of anything. Like Lorca too, he began by writing poetry which owes something to folksong and children's rhymes, but more to the venerable Spanish tradition of incorporating the freshness and simplicity of such songs into cultivated literature. His first book, *Marinero en tierra* (1924), written while he was in poor health in and near Madrid, is full of playful grace and nonsense rhymes; but the waves and boats of Cadiz bay which call to the landlocked Alberti belong to a childhood and freedom he has lost, and his wish to sink and drift in the submarine gardens of the mother of life hint at a nostalgia for something that reaches back beyond childhood itself. However, the note of personal melancholy is no more than a faint undertone, and disappears completely in *La amante* (1926), his poetic record of an actual excursion by car from Madrid to the north coast and back. Little poems of extreme simplicity echo traditional songs and make carefree comment on what Alberti sees before his eyes. It is very delicately done, but quite trivial. A festive tone still prevails in his third book, *El alba del alhelí* (1927), but his style and his moods are beginning to grow more complicated. As well as simple Andalusian love-songs, there are poems whose imagery and concepts strive for ingenuity; others, like his ironic self-portrait, 'El tonto de Rafael', display a truculent desire to shock and nonplus which anticipates the crazy, silent-film humour of his *Yo era un tonto y lo que he visto me ha hecho dos tontos* of 1929.

But a more radical change took place in *Cal y canto* (1929), written during 1926 and 1927 under the double influence of Góngora whom Alberti admired at this time more fervently than any of his friends, and of his interest in *ultraísmo*. In most poems he prudently

keeps these two disparate (though not absolutely incompatible) styles
apart. His Gongorine poems, which include a 'Soledad tercera',
pursue a difficult beauty in a rarefied realm of intricate images and
concepts which demand patient reflection and careful deciphering.
Other poems, of quite a different kind, stun the reader with baffling
scenes from the breathless, cacophonous world of modern times.
Alberti, however, is less inclined than the *ultraístas* to glorify it, and
hints rather at its fragmented incoherence and coldness. Occasionally
he brings the two styles together, or at any rate explores with Gongorine subtlety rather than *ultraísta* shock tactics such things as the
world of the cinema, or the grace and glory of a famous goalkeeper.
If art for art's sake means anything, it means Alberti's *Cal y canto*
and his way of taking any subject—a telegram, a drunken sailor—as
a pretext for displaying his total command of rich poetic resources.

When Alberti finished *Cal y canto* he was still only twenty-five. At
this age he was quite suddenly overwhelmed by an intense emotional
crisis, aggravated by illness, whose origins he has described at some
length, if not very precisely, in *La arboleda perdida* (1959). It is
amazing that this collapse into a private hell of despair and nausea
did not destroy his poetic impetus; but on the contrary, his agonised
determination to chart his terrible experience produced his greatest
book, *Sobre los ángeles* (1929). Unlike Lorca, whose season in hell
sufficiently disturbed his creative control to throw up the many
impenetrable private images of *Poeta en Nueva York*, Alberti's self-
discipline is rarely shaken; however deeply introspective his lament,
he does not lose sight of the fact that his purpose is to communicate
it to others. Naturally, poems which seek to reach deep into the
sensation of being a broken, walking corpse in a filthy, shattered,
hostile world, do not make easy reading. Furthermore, the book,
which begins with a poem entitled 'Paraíso perdido', contains many
references to Alberti's childhood and education in the Jesuit college
of the Puerto, so we may expect to find personal associations not
readily intelligible to everyone.[13] But the difficulties are rarely in-
superable. *Sobre los ángeles* is no more surrealistic than the Book of
Revelation, and it is a good deal more explicit. The titles of the
poems invariably indicate their themes with sufficient clarity. The
angels of most of the poems represent forces governing different
facets or moods of Alberti's inner nature as he now sees it, and his
reactions to the world outside, so that each angel concentrates the
poet's attention on one aspect of his spiritual state or one zone of

reminiscence about his past life. This attention is then clothed in formidable metaphors of bitterness, revulsion, nostalgia—and occasionally hope and peace, for there are also good angels—which certainly tax the imagination, but also invite the reader to share and understand a remarkable experience. The experience itself is not a pleasant one. Alberti was physically ill, and his unhappiness brought him to the verge of mental breakdown. But his poetic intelligence and vision remained unimpaired. As a result he was able to transform a personal catastrophe into some of the most powerful and imaginative Spanish poetry of the century.

The extraordinarily wholehearted way in which this generation dedicated themselves to poetry in the twenties tended to fade in all of them at the end of the decade. In 1930 Alberti published a kind of postscript to *Sobre los ángeles*, called *Sermones y moradas*. Its themes are the same, the freedom of metrical structure which he had adopted in *Sobre los ángeles* now becomes total, and poetry overlaps with prose. But the power and urgency of the former book has diminished; it is as if Alberti had come to terms with his crisis but wished to squeeze another book out of it. From 1930 onwards his poetic work was crowded out by political activities. In 1931 he joined the Communist Party, and worked busily for the cause during the Republic and the war. Although the propaganda poetry he wrote —and has continued to write—has been rightly judged greatly inferior to his other work, it is only fair to remember that it is occasional poetry in the strict sense of the word. Most of the verse he wrote during the Civil War was composed for his recitals to troops in the field, recitals which are remembered with gratitude and emotion by hard-bitten commanders like Lister. In exile, Alberti's work has been varied and uneven, the best of it being *A la pintura* (1952), which makes sensitive poetry out of his considerable talent as a painter and out of his love of painting, and *Retornos de lo vivo lejano* (1952), poems of dignified nostalgia which regain something of the depth and strength of the best of his pre-war work.

Luis Cernuda (1902-63), although three months older than Alberti, was slower to make his mark as a poet. Family reasons kept him in Seville until 1928, and he had little direct contact with other poets except Salinas, who was his teacher at Seville University. His first published book of poems, *Perfil del Aire* (1927), was not well received, and was dismissed by some as imitations of Guillén.

Cernuda at this time was a morbidly shy introvert, and the frustrations of his early years bred deep resentments which were later to show both in his poetry and his writings about his contemporaries. *Perfil del Aire* (which he revised and called *Primeras poesías* in 1936), resembles *Cántico*, however, only in elegant artistry and its Classical forms. Its themes, like those the 'Égloga', 'Elegía', and 'Oda' which followed it in 1928, are melancholy, and reveal Cernuda as yet another poet responsive to the myth of a lost paradise, replaced by a prison-like reality of 'hastío', solitude, and beauty that blooms only to wither and die; in this reality Cernuda feels condemned to the special torment of aspiring to an ideal and eternal world which he knows he can never attain. Though the form of this poetry looks to the literature of the Golden Age, the sentiments are exactly those of Bécquer.

In 1928 he was at last able to leave Seville for Madrid, and then for Toulouse, where he taught for a year before returning to Madrid. At this time he became interested in surrealist theory, which on his own admission affected his next three books of poetry, *Un río, un amor, Los placeres prohibidos,* and *Donde habite el olvido,* written between 1929 and 1933. This did not mean, any more than it did for Lorca or even Aleixandre, that he unconditionally surrendered his art to the unedited voice of his subconscious. What appealed to him most in surrealism was its wholehearted rebellion not merely against artistic conventions, but against all the norms of a society which Cernuda found despicable and hostile—as he affirmed with extraordinary virulence in the 'Poética' he wrote for the first edition of Diego's anthology. Surrealist freedom offered the opportunity for greater self-honesty—always a matter of prime importance for Cernuda—for greater liberty to say what he found when he looked into himself, particularly since his findings, like the strange associations of his prose-poems or the homosexuality of his painful love-poetry, did not make for conventional reading. *Un río, un amor* and *Los placeres prohibidos* achieve moments of joyful experience of love and beauty, but they are overshadowed by a more powerful sense of loneliness and inner void, and by a further statement of the theme that was to provide the title for Cernuda's collected poetic work, *La realidad y el deseo*: reality is a prison from which he cannot escape to realise the ideal aspirations which he cannot suppress, and which seem to him to be the lingering intimations of a lost paradise. Few poets have lived out the myth of the Fall with such real personal pain as Cernuda. *Donde habite el olvido* (the title comes from Bécquer) forms a melancholy postscript to the other two books, in a calmer, clearer tone of disillusion. It speaks of the death of love, and of the love of death, as a final escape, as the Romantics saw it, into something truer and less equivocal than life. Cernuda is also conscious of his special and inescapable calling as a poet, and this becomes an important theme of his next poems, *Invocaciones*. Again, the echoes of Bécquer are strong. One of the causes of his sense of solitude is having to live in 'esta sucia tierra donde el poeta se ahoga'.

Cernuda's poetry manifests an unusual combination of forces which hold it in a state of perpetual tension. His attitude to the world around him and his idea of the Poet's place in it have caused many readers to regard him as a genuine Romantic. His resemblance to Bécquer in this respect is indeed striking, but it is not the whole of Cernuda. Although his sense of alienation from a hostile, bourgeois world urges him to escape from it, through art, in pursuit of a paradise he vaguely recalls and still fleetingly perceives, he will not ignore the fact that as well as 'deseo' his life is concerned with 'realidad', and that it is also his task to make sense of the latter, or at least to define and explore his response to it. The Civil War changed his reality bewilderingly. In spite of his desire to be of service to the Republican cause, he remained a mere onlooker, mainly from abroad, and his poems of the period, *Las nubes*, although they reflect feelings provoked by the conflict, are not about the war. Thereafter he spent fourteen years in Britain, living a quiet, grey life on the margin of reality, reading a great deal—notably Hölderlin, in whom he recognised a kindred spirit, and English poetry (and criticism, which, he said, taught him to excise the pathetic fallacy and the purple passage from his work), and adding steadily to the body of poetry which in successive editions of 1936, 1940, and 1958 continued to bear the title *La realidad y el deseo*. The subjects of his poetry, like the title, remain the same, but he develops a mature versatility of style, and a growing concern to speak directly and clearly about his life and circumstances. Many of the poems of *Vivir sin estar viviendo*, written between 1944 and 1949, present sensitive poetic insights in plain, at times almost prosaic, language, and the result is a gain in strength. Cernuda is also achieving something like serenity. While he never ceases to believe that his demanding vocation as a poet means suffering and solitude, some of his poems affirm almost contentedly the rewards of his high calling, the visionary moments which, though they are only moments, seem like glimpses of eternity and the lost paradise.

In 1952, after teaching for five years in Massachusetts, he moved to Mexico, where, during vacations from his teaching, he had fallen deeply and happily in love. His last years were fruitful, in literary studies, poetic prose, and poetry. *Con las horas contadas,* which completed the 1958 edition of *La realidad y el deseo,* often speaks in clear tones of the joy he finds, in moments of love and beauty, and in his servitude to poetry. Cernuda had one more book of poetry to write before he died, and it is perhaps his finest of all: *Desolación de la Quimera* (1962). It is very clearly the work of a man of great personal integrity preparing himself for death, setting the record straight as regards his attitude to life, to art, to his country, and to himself. There are no recantations or apologies to be made. Cernuda has not found paradise, or God, he has not forgiven his enemies, nor bourgeois society's hypocrisy and repulsive conventions (marriage, the family), and he wants no contact with '. . . esa España obscena y deprimente / En la que regentea hoy la canalla'. In the magnificent poem which bears the title of the whole volume, he reaffirms his belief that the rewards of the poet's divine madness are inevitably 'la aridez, la ruina y la muerte'. But Cernuda faces all this steadily, and with a dignity that illuminates and justifies the quiet confidence of his simple statement: 'He aprendido / El oficio de hombre duramente'.

The pre-eminence of the six poets considered so far ought not to obscure the fact that this was a prolific, as well as a brilliant, period for Spanish poetry. But space permits only a brief reminder that interesting and excellent poems were written by others who did not reach or sustain the heights of their greater contemporaries.

Gerardo Diego (1896-   ) is remembered chiefly today for his extremely important anthologies of modern Spanish poetry, but he was a considerable poet in his own right. A poet of quite astonishing versatility, within the space of a few years he produced collections as different as the sensitive evocations of *Soria* (1923), the *ultraísta* fun and games of *Imagen* (1922), which took on a more specifically *creacionista* character—after he had met Huidobro in Paris—in the aptly named *Manual de espumas* (1924), and the calm lyricism of *Versos humanos* (1925). *Imagen* and *Manual de espumas* may not be his best books, but they are possibly the most important. Their exuberant espousal of total poetic (and typographical) freedom and their dedication to the autonomy of art—the poems are fragmented bundles of images which refer to nothing outside themselves—paved the way for other poets to make more interesting use of fantasy and surprise in the twenties. Diego's experiments may also represent the least flimsy memorials to the fashionable poetic -isms of the period. Many of their mental acrobatics are imaginative and amusing, though it is difficult not to grow weary under a prolonged bombardment. His later poetry is more conventional and more substantial. *Ángeles de Compostela* (1940) and the sonnets of *Alondra de verdad* (1943) rarely rise far above the humdrum, but they are always fluent and sometimes moving, and did something to relieve the desolate state of Spanish poetry during the years immediately after the Civil War.

Emilio Prados (1899-1962) is limited in a different way. Far from having squandered his talents in an entertaining display of versatility, he confines them to the exploration of a private, inner world where there is little invitation to the reader to follow him. A sad and rather solitary man, whose refusal to permit any of his poems to appear in the 1934 edition of Diego's anthology is symptomatic of his attitude to the matter of communication, he used his art, as did Jiménez and Cernuda, to unravel what was for him the mysterious relation between his inner world and the outer world of nature. His early books, such as *Tiempo* (1925), *Vuelta* (1927), *Memoria de poesía* (1927), and *Cuerpo perseguido* (1928), show him to have been capable of writing stronger, deeper poetry than Diego ever produced. But his verse rarely manages—or even seems to want—to involve the reader in its mournful self-questioning; and unlike Jiménez and Cernuda, Prados makes no progress with his problems. Although he came out of his shell and participated sufficiently in political activity during the Republic to have to go into exile in 1939, the poetry he wrote in Mexico after the war—*Jardín cerrado* (1946), *La piedra escrita* (1961), *Signos del ser* (1962)—returns to his pre-war themes, with a deepened nostalgia and more broodings on death and oblivion.

Manuel Altolaguirre (1905-59), like his inseparable friend Prados, was from Málaga, where the pair of them made literary history by founding and publishing the magazine *Litoral*, in which much of the early work of the best poets of the generation first saw the light between 1927 and 1929. Altolaguirre's own poetry, as he says in his 'Poética' in Diego's anthology, derives directly from Jiménez. Like Jiménez and Prados, he presents himself in his poems as a sad and solitary man, a kind of low-powered Platonist who looks at nature with the eyes of the soul, and makes private contact with essences behind the surface of things. But Altolaguirre employs more modest poetic resources than Jiménez to convey his wistful visions, and there is no sense of struggle either with concepts or language. A delicate sensibility of what is mysterious in nature and in himself is expressed in eminently unmysterious, adequate images and symbols: a somewhat unusual combination at this period, but one that did not prevent Altolaguirre from writing some very readable poetry, though like Prados, whom he accompanied into exile in 1939, he found little new to say after the war.

Of the many lesser poets who flourished in this fertile age, the two who are most likely to survive as more than names in anthologies or manuals of literature are León Felipe (1884-1968) and Miguel Hernández (1910-42). Felipe's uncompromising individualism, together with the wanderlust, and subsequently the political convictions, which caused him to spend forty-five of his eighty-four years outside Spain—though without ceasing to be preoccupied with his own Spanishness—set him apart from all literary fashions and tendencies, and his work is far better known in Mexico than in Spain. His rugged, honest, Whitmanesque poetry is very much a matter of taste, but it addresses itself directly and powerfully to a wide audience, and is unlikely to be forgotten.

Hernández's work is much more difficult to assess. Nurtured and encouraged by the poets of the Generation of 1927, his poetry clearly marks a transition from their own to a new poetic era, and his influence on post-war poetry has been considerable. But his work is so thickly encrusted with legends that are still very much alive that it is hard to know whether one is responding to what it reflects of Hernández's singular personal history, or to a poetic achievement which will outlive the emotions at present inseparable from his memory. Although the poverty and illiteracy of the young Hernández have sometimes been exaggerated, he was indeed an untutored goatherd when he felt the first stirrings of the desire to become a poet, and his first, deliberate, self-imposed task was to learn to write cultured poetry. The result was *Perito en lunas* (1933), a polished, stylised, and rather sterile exercise in the manner of Góngora. As a proof that the ex-goatherd could master poetic forms and rhetorical ingenuity it was an undoubted success. But it was only an exercise, and it lacks the modern and personal stamp which a poet like Alberti put on his Gongorine poetry. Hernández's next book of poems, *El rayo que no cesa* (1936), is very different in many respects, and suggests that there was another crisis through which Hernández had to struggle in order to develop as a poet. *El rayo que no cesa* reveals, as *Perito en lunas* did not, that he was a man of intense, explosive passions and impulses which constantly threatened to burst out uncontrollably. He was, as he says in one of the poems, 'una revolución dentro de un hueso, / un rayo soy sujeto a una redoma'. The principal theme of the book is love, but Hernández's moods range through realms of rapture, rage, suffering, despair, and black premonitions of death. Either because of a conscious need to discipline his seething emotions, or as a further exercise in technical skills, he forces his passion into strict Classical forms, though looking less to Góngora now than to Garcilaso and Lope de Vega. It is a most uneasy combination, at worst embarrassingly so; the book still belongs to Hernández's literary apprenticeship, from which he began to emerge after writing it, leaning less heavily on approved models and developing confidence in his capacity to express his feelings more directly. For some years, excessive emotionalism still represented a constant peril in his poetry, however. His 'Elegía' to Ramón Sijé, one of his best-known poems, commands respect as a sincere outpouring of grief on the sudden death of a dear friend. But if such human sympathy is put aside, parts of the poem are almost ridiculously florid. Another widely admired poem of this period, 'Sino sangrento', mixes some absurdly melodramatic rhetoric into its attempt to convey a sense of tragic fate; again, human considerations and Hernández's 'legend' intervene, for the grim prophecy of a bloody destiny was to be tragically fulfilled almost immediately.

During the Republic, the young Hernández was impulsively, but totally and sincerely, converted from fervent Catholicism to fervent communism, and when war broke out he served his beliefs both as a fighting soldier and a poet. Although the war poems collected in *Viento del pueblo* (1937) can rarely be described as propagandist, many of them were written, like Alberti's war poetry, to be recited to his fellow-soldiers. They express many moods, from raging fury to gentle compassion, and though it is in some ways a regrettable observation to have to make, the experience of war and its suffering was unquestionably beneficial to Hernández's poetry, purging it of rhetorical artifice and of over-dramatisation of his sentiments. A second book resulting from the war, *El hombre acecha* (1938), is more personal and reflective than *Viento del pueblo,* and speaks quietly and simply of his suffering and sadness, which he naturally sees reflected in his companions.

At the end of the war Hernández was captured, imprisoned, and sentenced to death. He died of tuberculosis, still a political prisoner, at the age of thirty-one. The poems he wrote in prison during the last three years of his life, collected as *Cancionero y Romancero de ausencias*, are a noble and dignified lament which needs no artifice to make it deeply moving. No reader can fail to respond to this record of a brave man's unremitting suffering, separated from the beloved wife and child he was never to see again, and deprived of the light and air and simple joys of a country life which had never ceased to afford him solace. In these poems Hernández clearly stands at the beginning of what would have been a new phase in his poetic development, though the transition was not an abrupt one. Even the simplest of the poems he wrote in prison are much less artless and spontaneous than some commentators would have us believe. He still works ingeniously with metaphor and symbol, and his poetry still taxes the imagination in a way that distinguishes it clearly from the equally moving letters he wrote to his wife from prison. What is new, and what has made his last poetry influential since the war, is that whether or not his poetic resources and techniques are in some way inferior to the human sentiment they express, they are inseparable from it in a way that poetry had not been since Bécquer. The legend of the illiterate shepherd's Gongorine subtleties, the anecdote and political passion, will eventually drop away from Hernández's last, best poetry; but its impact will still depend on the reader's identification with the human emotions it expresses. In the fifteen years since Ortega's *Deshumanización del arte*, the wheel had come full circle. In Hernández's poetry, the 'human interest' which Ortega had declared incompatible with aesthetic worth, and whose disappearance he had prophesied, returns to the centre of poetic art.

NOTES

1. L. Cernuda, *Estudios sobre poesía española contemporánea* (Madrid, 1957), p. 85.

2. Numerals refer to the number of the poem in any edition of Machado's *Poesías completas*.

3. See D. Alonso, *Poetas españoles contemporáneos* (Madrid, 1958), pp. 140-46.

4. D. Alonso, *Cuatro poetas españoles* (Madrid, 1962), pp. 137-85.

5. *TA* references are to the number of the poem in Jiménez's own selection, *Tercera antolojía* (Madrid, 1957). Dates of individual books are also Jiménez's, and refer to the period when the poems were written, not to date of publication.

6. 'Soy, fui y seré platónico . . .', J. R. Jiménez, *La corriente infinita* (Madrid, 1961), p. 178.

7. P. R. Olson, *Circle of Paradox. Time and Essence in the Poetry of Juan Ramón Jiménez* (Baltimore, 1967), p. 19.

8. Cernuda, op. cit., pp. 89-101.

9. F. García Lorca, *Obras completas* (4th edn., Madrid, 1960), pp. 1563-4.

10. 'Comentarios al *Romancero gitano*', *RO*, 77 (1969), 129-37.

11. cf. J. M. Aguirre, 'El sonambulismo de García Lorca', *BHS*, XLIV (1967), 267-85.

12. *Obras completas*, pp. 36-48.

13. See G. W. Connell, 'The Autobiographical Element in *Sobre los ángeles*', *BHS*, XL (1963), 160-73.

Chapter 3

DRAMA

IN THE TWENTIETH CENTURY, drama is unquestionably the branch
of the arts in which Spain has least to offer to the common store of
European culture. This is not due to a lack of original talent, but to
the great vitality and impregnable bourgeois vulgarity of the commercial stage throughout the period. Although interesting plays were
written, they were hardly ever successfully staged. The living theatre
resisted and discouraged the twentieth century's tendencies towards
experimental and minority art, and no latter-day Calderón arose to
produce great literature that also pleased the groundlings. While it
was not to be expected that writers like Unamuno, Valle-Inclán, and
Azorín would take the commercial theatre by storm, they belong to a
period when the work of Ibsen, Chekhov, Shaw, Maeterlinck,
Claudel, Giraudoux, and Pirandello was achieving some measure of
the acclaim so essential to this most public of the arts. But on the
Spanish stage, writers of this calibre were almost totally eclipsed by
an inexhaustible succession of monstrously fecund popular playwrights who had the knack of giving audiences exactly what they
wanted.

At the turn of the century, Spanish theatres were thriving on
Regency society's frenzied appetite for entertainment. The playgoing
set of Madrid's mere half-million inhabitants could choose every
night from at least eight well-run and well-patronised theatres.
Although the relatively limited numbers of the public usually meant
quite short runs even for successful plays, there was never any
shortage of acceptable material. The theatregoers were essentially
Echegaray's public, fashionable upper middle-class society, predominantly female and middle-aged. The influential critics of established daily and weekly periodicals were normally on the public's
side, and understood their job as advising playwrights how to please
the customers. It was imperative to entertain, but plays did not have

to be merely amusing. Moving the audience to tears, or even righteous indignation, was perfectly permissible. What good taste would not admit was any attempt to puzzle or worry the audience, or to reflect any moral or social values other than those of the bejewelled matrons of the orchestra stalls.

The angry young men of Azorín's generation inevitably found the state of the theatre as deplorable as every other aspect of the Spanish cultural and social scene at the end of the century. They were ready to make it one more battlefield in their generational conflict, and to subject drama to reform and experiment. But whereas in other genres real innovations and changes of direction were achieved, the impact of this generation on the theatre was very small. In 1905, when the press organised a national tribute to Echegaray, a group of writers which included Unamuno, Darío, Azorín, Baroja, Valle-Inclán, Antonio and Manuel Machado, Maeztu, and Jacinto Grau, signed a manifesto of public protest. It was a bold gesture which seemed to promise much for the future. But in retrospect, as far as the living theatre was concerned, it turns out to have been a last stand before they were decisively routed. The list of signatories is impressive, but more significant for the development of Spanish drama is that those on the list who tried writing for the stage themselves notably failed to please or interest the public. In the complete list of some fifty signatures, only Villaespesa, and to a lesser extent the Machado brothers, were to achieve any success in the theatre. On the other hand, the names of the playwrights whom the public were to take to their heart are conspicuously absent from the list.

Nevertheless, within the narrow limits prescribed by popular taste, some changes were taking place at the turn of the century. The nineties, although dominated by the still vigorous Echegaray, witnessed theatrical stirrings which make it reasonable to look for some kind of watershed at about this period. One event which on the face of it might seem to mark a new departure was the first performance, in October 1895, of Joaquín Dicenta's *Juan José*. Dicenta (1863-1917) had hitherto been known as a bohemian personality and the author of poorly written sentimental melodramas such as *El suicidio de Werther* (1888) and *La honra y la vida* (1889). But *Juan José* turned him into a famous playwright. The protagonist of the new play was an illiterate, illegitimate member of the industrial poor, who loses his job, takes to robbery, goes to prison, and breaks out to murder his overseer and cause the death of his mistress.

Since this sad tale is presented as that of a noble, helpless victim of social circumstances and possibly of capitalist exploitation, *Juan José* has been regarded by some as a 'proletarian' play, ushering in a new era of socially committed drama. The immediate and enormous success of the play with fashionable audiences, however, suggests otherwise. Its initial run of forty-one performances—extraordinary success by contemporary standards—was followed by frequent revivals which show how rapidly it became an established favourite. Whatever Dicenta's intention, the consensus of current opinion saw the play for what it undoubtedly was: another sentimental melodrama of jealousy and honour. Eduardo Bustillo's enthusiastic review in the conservative *Ilustración española y americana* (15 November 1895) repeatedly describes the play as 'hermoso'. He applauds Dicenta's awareness that passionate sentiment may be discovered even in the lowest social classes, and, without any tendentious intent, makes the very valid point that Juan José's workmate in the play, although subject to the same social and economic pressures, has no dramatic problem, simply because his mistress is a good girl, loyal to her man, and more resigned to poverty and hardship than Juan José's flighty and comfort-loving Rosa.

After *Juan José*, Dicenta continued to toy with social drama. It is feasible to argue that *El señor feudal* (1897) goes much further than *Juan José* in venturing to express social attitudes that did not correspond with those of the typical theatre audience.[1] Historically, however, such an argument is of little importance. Dicenta continued to be admired and remembered as the author of *Juan José*, and not as the founder of a new kind of drama. By the end of the century it was clear that *El señor feudal* did not foreshadow the lines along which Spanish drama was to develop. By that time, in fact, the most successful lines of development had already been determined by certain circumstances in the early career of the dramatist who was to dominate the Spanish stage for more than half a century, Jacinto Benavente (1866-1954).

In spite of his longevity and prodigious productivity, Benavente's early years and works are his most important ones, at least from the point of view of literary history. If anyone could have revitalised drama as his contemporaries revitalised poetry and the novel, it was Benavente. In 1894, when his first play, *El nido ajeno*, was performed in Madrid, he clearly saw that the times were ripe for change. He

was twenty-eight, well educated, travelled, knowledgeable about the
theatre in all its aspects, from the history of European drama to the
technical business of mounting a good professional production. He
was also sufficiently a member of his generation of liberal intellectuals to be concerned about the cultural decadence of Spain. Lists of
members of the Generation of 1898 usually include his name. Yet
he differed from his distinguished contemporaries in important
respects from the beginning of his career, and it is significant that
in 1905, with a decade of theatrical experience behind him, he did
not sign the anti-Echegaray manifesto. The development of his work
during that decade suggests that he consciously faced a choice
between being a successful playwright and a misunderstood genius,
and had decided to be a successful playwright.

   El nido ajeno, though not the best, is perhaps the most serious
play Benavente ever wrote. Its basic theme, the role of married
women in middle-class society, was as much a matter of topical
concern in Spain towards the end of the century as it had been in
northern Europe when Ibsen dealt with it. Moreover, Benavente
observes with some perspicacity the specifically Spanish aspects of
the problem—the way in which a senseless residue of conventions
regarding matrimonial honour can trivialise and stultify the life of
an intelligent, sociable, and entirely honourable married woman. On
the Madrid stage, the play was a catastrophic failure. It was taken
off after three days amid a clamour of disapproval. What the critics
(the same critics who thought *Juan José* so 'hermoso' the following
year) found most disgustingly offensive was a scene in which two
brothers discuss the possibility that their mother had been unfaithful
to their father. The critic of *El Imparcial* (7 October 1894), boiling
with indignation and embarrassment, asserted that this kind of thing
was not only absolutely inadmissible on the stage, but totally
unrealistic.

   It is easy to imagine the dilemma of the young Benavente. In a
sense, public reaction had proved to the hilt how urgent was the
need to penetrate the Cloud-cuckoo-land of the Spanish theatre with
this kind of play. Yet what future was there likely to be in trying
to reform the theatre with plays that would be booed off the stage?
His second effort, *Gente conocida* of 1896, shows him feeling his
way towards some kind of honourable compromise. Instead of the
intense soul-searching of *El nido ajeno,* the new play consisted of a
series of more or less static, urbane conversation-pieces, which portray

5   *   *

the hypocrisy, materialism, and petty malevolence of polite society. There is little action until the final act, when the young daughter of a cynical new-rich factory-owner, who has arranged her marriage to a bankrupt, morally disreputable, but impeccably noble duke, rebels in the name of personal decency against the shifty accommodations and deceits of this nasty little gathering of all the best people. *Gente conocida* ran for ten days, and there were no complaints about offensive subject-matter. Evidently the critics and the public did not see any important values menaced here. The play's social criticism was sharp, but no longer 'unrealistic'—that is to say, unthinkable. It stopped well short of criticising the existing social structure. Even the ruined dukes in the audience could at least approve of Benavente's treatment of factory-owners.

After the comparative success of *Gente conocida*, Benavente continued to exploit this vein of innocuous but not entirely irresponsible social satire. *La comida de las fieras* (1898) sustains the unexceptionable thesis that while one is rich, smart, and hospitable, one may rule polite society as a lion-tamer rules his animals, and even induce the beasts to make friendly gestures. But if the tamer's authority falters (in this case, as a result of bad luck on the Stock Exchange), the animals will at once devour their master with rare ferocity. An appendix to the main action shows that the protagonists are much happier after they have been ruined, ostracised, and slandered by the smart society whose adulation they once enjoyed. Further plays of this kind followed in rapid succession, and were increasingly applauded by the society they castigated. In 1903 Benavente extended his sardonic gaze to European aristocracy at large, and, in *La noche del sábado*, concluded that moral degradation and hypocrisy among the privileged classes—together with unexpected sparks of decency, authenticity, and vigour—are not confined to Spain. *La noche del sábado* is one of Benavente's most exotic plays, encompassing the glittering society of imperial princes and the lurid, grotesque underworld of circus life. After murder and tragedy, the play ends on a note of high passion. It is an undeniably polished piece of writing, which already demonstrates both the strengths and limitations of Benavente's drama. The action is crowded into the end of the play, and verges on melodrama in the sense that the audience has not been psychologically prepared for such a violent outcome. Fundamentally it is a spectacular collage of conversations which spell out the vague, worldly-wise thesis of *Gente conocida*, and it was a decided success in 1903. Benavente had mastered both the knack of pleasing Spanish audiences and the formula of writing social satires which offended nobody. From now on, with growing confidence, he extended his range. *Señora ama* (1908) and *La malquerida* (1913) use rural settings, one for an ironical sketch of provincial *mores* and the other for a somewhat steamy rustic melodrama which is nevertheless one of his most powerful works. Other plays make use of historical or allegorical material. But by 1903 his dramatic talents were already fully developed, and although he continued to write successfully for the stage until the end of his long life, the aims and style of his work remained substantially unchanged. The convention of selecting the relatively early *Los intereses creados* (1907) as one of his best and most characteristic plays is perfectly justified. A light, fast-moving comedy of intrigue, smoothly blending elements from the *commedia dell'arte* with others from Spanish Golden Age drama, *Los intereses creados* gaily reiterates Benavente's cynical thesis that human beings are eminently corruptible and hypocritical, and society is like a puppet-show where the strings that move the dolls are usually coarse bonds of material ambitions. As ever, this cheerless moral is partly relieved by an isolated instance of sincere feeling. We are informed at the end that among the strings there is a delicate thread of true love, which brings a hint of divinity to the otherwise squalid spectacle. But this fugitive happy thought is demolished in a sequel to the play where we learn that Leandro's love did not long survive the tedium of marriage.

By the time he wrote *Los intereses creados*, Benavente's conquest of a large popular audience was beginning to cause some unease among his more intellectual contemporaries. They had thought he was one of them. Juan Ramón Jiménez had once called him a prince of the new renaissance of Spanish letters. Yet it was an article of faith, as Ortega reminded Spaniards in 1908, that 'hoy . . es imposible que una labor de alta literatura logre reunir público suficiente para sustentarse'.[2] But it was the ideological schism provoked in Spain in the First World War which brought antagonism between Benavente and the intellectuals to a head. 'Intellectuals' is a term that can be used here with almost absurd precision, for in the angry debates between pro-German traditionalists and pro-Allied liberals, the word was used simply to identify a writer or artist of pro-Allied sympathies. The matter was so clear-cut that Benavente, whose conservatism made him pro-German, suddenly found that he was neither an intellectual nor an artist, and was being ostracised by most Spanish writers of any importance. The gulf between him and the intellectuals has had important consequences for the Spanish theatre. 1916 saw the first performance of his *La ciudad alegre y confiada,* a sequel to *Los intereses creados,* but also a bitterly polemical treatment of the subject of Spain and the European war. It asserts aggressively reactionary values, and not only ridicules the snobbish practitioners of 'hermetic' art, but suggests that their cowardice and introspective pessimism is playing into the hands of sinister left-wing demagogues whose aim is to betray Spain's noblest patriotic ideals and traditions.

Since the days when Pérez de Ayala inveighed (in the reviews and essays collected in *Las máscaras*) against the 'valor negativo' that Benavente represented for the theatre, critics have continued to pour scorn on his efforts, and to regard his popularity as a sort of national disgrace. He has been accused of triviality, of coldness, of having failed to reflect the reality of Spanish society. There is substance in all these criticisms, although in part they rebuke Benavente for failing to be what he never wanted to be, at any rate after *El nido ajeno.* Yet within the confines of his small world, he displays considerable sophistication. His wit bites sharply, if not deeply, and his attitude to the section of society that chiefly interested him is consistently critical. He was not the bourgeoisie's tame jester; indeed he may well have managed to educate them to some small degree, and to make them aware of some of their more unpleasant characteristics.

Lesser men prospered in Benavente's shadow. Manuel Linares Rivas (1878-1938) has today passed into oblivion, but in his time his bourgeois thesis-dramas such as *La garra* (1914), defending divorce against clerical obscurantism, and *La fuerza del mal* (1914), brought him fame, fortune, and Academician's laurels. The reputation of Gregorio Martínez Sierra (1881-1948) also stood high both in Spain and abroad during the first quarter of the century. A busy literary man, poet, novelist, journalist, translator, actor-manager-producer, he is mainly remembered for exceedingly sentimental plays like *Canción de cuna* (1911), *Mamá* (1912), and *Madame Pepita* (1912). What attaches him to the Benavente school of bourgeois drama is his realism and the faint suggestion of thesis in his plays—for example, in *Canción de cuna,* a timid insistence on the frustrated maternal instincts of nuns. The predominance of female characters in Martínez

Sierra's plays, his general preoccupation with asserting the dignity of Spanish motherhood, and a tepid adherence to the feminist cause, lend support to the widespread belief that some of his writing was actually done by his wife.

The popularity of the *alta comedia*—as realistic bourgeois drama had been called since the days of López de Ayala—did not mean that Benavente and his followers exercised exclusive dominion over the Spanish stage at this time. Two distinctly different types of theatre won different measures of public approval: the so-called *teatro poético,* and the heterogeneous sub-genre of *costumbrista* comedy.

Teatro poético is an imprecise and potentially misleading term. It may be taken to refer, and sometimes does refer, to an attempt to carry *modernismo* into the theatre, and to offer, as an alternative to the actuality of Dicenta's taverns and Benavente's drawing-rooms, escape into an artificial world of poetic fantasy. Such an attempt was made: principally, as far as theatre audiences of the time were concerned, by the poet Francisco Villaespesa, who achieved considerable success with rhymed plays of extravagant passion in exotic settings—Moorish Spain in *Abén Humeya* (1914) and *El alcázar de las perlas* (1911), medieval in *Doña María de Padilla* (1913) and *El Rey Galaor* (1913). Such plays were not universally admired even in their day. In the preface to the third edition of *Las máscaras,* Pérez de Ayala says that he has tried to lighten the tone of his essays 'con el contraste y respiro de un tema cómico, como lo es siempre un drama poético del señor Villaespesa', and while some champions have come forward to defend Benavente against Pérez de Ayala's criticism, posterity has unanimously confirmed his rude dismissal of Villaespesa.

The most popular exponent of *teatro poético,* however, was Eduardo Marquina (1879-1946). His plays are of a distinctly different kind from the *modernista* vapourings of Villaespesa, and the convention of attaching the label to Marquina makes it clear that *teatro poético* means simply verse drama, and could perfectly well include the rhymed plays of Echegaray, or, for that matter, Zorrilla and García Gutiérrez. Marquina had written lyric poetry in the modernist style during the first years of the century, but he made his reputation with plays like *Las hijas del Cid* (1908) and *En Flandes se ha puesto el sol* (1910). These are historical dramas, and, far from representing a new orientation in the Spanish theatre, are imitations of Romantic imitations of Golden Age historical plays. The only modern note is the melancholy tint of the strong vein of patriotic sentiment in Marquina's plays. *Las hijas del Cid* attempts to stir the souls of his compatriots with an evocation of their long-vanished national hero; *En Flandes se ha puesto el sol*, a thin and rather foolish tale of divided loyalties, also seeks to evoke the glorious spirit of Spanish military men of the seventeenth century, but it is pointedly set in the era when Spanish dominion of the Netherlands was nearing its end, and in this respect reflects something of the national pessimism of the Generation of 1898.

If *teatro poético* simply means verse drama, it must include Manuel and Antonio Machado's efforts to apply their poetic gifts, in collaboration, to the theatre. A considerable number of plays, sometimes on historical or legendary themes—*Desdichas de la fortuna* (1926), *Juan de Mañara* (1927)—sometimes using popular material—*La Lola se va a los puertos* (1930)—do nothing to add to the reputation of either of the brothers, and contribute nothing to the development of Spanish drama. *Teatro poético* must also include the verse drama of José María Pemán (1898-). Although much of his work belongs chronologically to the post-Civil War period, his style is distinctly and deliberately old-fashioned, and bears no mark of the influence of the dramatic experiments of the late twenties and thirties. Pemán is that rather rare bird in Spain, a serious, committed dramatist of the Catholic Right. His best verse drama is historical—*El divino impaciente* (1933), *Cisneros* (1934), *La santa virreina* (1939)—and seeks to reaffirm on the modern stage what he believes to be Spain's most solid and admirable traditional values. As a distinguished public figure, former President of the Real Academia, and a well-known journalist, Pemán has always been able to count on a good reception for his plays.

A third kind of entertainment of which the public approved was much more confident in its patriotic fervour than was the nostalgia for better days expressed by Marquina and Pemán, and bears witness to the fact that the Generation of 1898 had failed to dissuade most Spaniards from their conviction that it was a great joy to be alive and Spanish in the twentieth century. By 1900, self-congratulatory *costumbrismo*, which in the days of Mesonero Romanos and Fernán Caballero had been founded on solemn pretensions to protect

Spaniards from ideological unrest, had become a thing of pure entertainment. On the stage, it was inseparably associated with musical comedy, and most specifically with the so-called *género chico*, the one-act *sainete*, usually part-spoken, part-sung, which had reached great heights of popularity towards the end of the nineteenth century with such works as *La Gran Vía* (1894) and the even more famous *La verbena de la Paloma* of the same year. Nearly all playwrights of the period had some contact with this hybrid genre. Dicenta, Marquina, even Benavente, wrote *libretti* for musical works. But whereas for them it was an occasional sideline, another group of writers drew their inspiration directly from the world of the *género chico* (and of the three-act *zarzuela*, from which the *género chico* derived) in order to produce more substantial and sometimes more serious drama than was offered by musical comedy.

To this group belong the brothers Serafín and Joaquín Álvarez Quintero (1871-1938 and 1873-1944), even though most of their work was not set to music. The essence of the *género chico* was its combination of lighthearted representation of popular *tipos* (in the venerable tradition of *pasos* and *entremeses*) and the *costumbrista* vision of a region or city as a picturesque spectacle of which Spaniards might feel justly proud. The Quinteros, born and bred in the province of Seville, moved to Madrid at an early age, and there presented, in play after play—some two hundred in all—dexterous, smoothly professional comedy which perpetuates the mythical Andalusia of Estébanez Calderón, a sunlit land of inexhaustible charm, grace, and wit, where no one can be really wicked, or miserably poor, or irremediably unhappy. This was a very pleasant view of things to have amid the turmoil and violence of twentieth-century Spain and Europe, and audiences responded with appropriate enthusiasm, both in Spain and abroad—for the Quinteros have supplied many an English amateur dramatic society with the sort of thing they expect of charming, colourful Andalusia.

Although the Quinteros made a huge success out of situating their skilfully contrived dramatic trivia in southern Spain, the favourite setting for folksy entertainment at this period was Madrid itself. The *género chico*, and the *zarzuela* proper, characteristically portray the gay life of the capital's idle poor. From this world of singing *chulos* and *majas* arose a writer who still provokes considerable differences of opinion, Carlos Arniches (1866-1943). He began as an author—or often co-author, for Spanish writers of this period were much given to collaboration when writing for the stage—of ordinary musical *sainetes*, and the small virtue of his early work is its trans- formation of authentic low-life repartee into amusing, vigorous stage dialogue. But about the time when Valle-Inclán decided that it was immoral for writers to go on 'playing at art' instead of fighting for social justice, Arniches too began to introduce a distinct note of social criticism into his work. The Madrid populace of his *sainetes*, formerly mere picturesque expressions of 'la gracia popular', became the object of his compassion and even indignation. At the same time, degraded, grotesque characters, anticipating the *esperpento*, started to appear in his plays.

Pérez de Ayala, who seized on Arniches as a stick to beat Bena- vente with, and praised all his work very highly, argued that his merit had been as great in the days when nobody took him seriously as in his later work. But there is a world of difference between his early, flippant, musical sketches and the black humour and social theses of his three-act dramas, such as *La señorita de Trevélez* (1916), *Los caciques* (1920), and *La heroica villa* (1921), all of which deal with life in the provinces. The first of these, Arniches's best play, considers the evils engendered by boredom, ignorance, and idiotic frivolity in a grim provincial capital. In this case the town is bluntly called Villanea, but readers acquainted with Alas's Vetusta, Pérez de Ayala's Pilares or Guadalfranco, Baroja's Castro Duro or Alcolea de Campo, know the place well enough. An elderly school- master is introduced purely for the purpose of pointing a moral about the criminal lack of education and civic responsibility among the citizens of such towns. But the personal drama of honour played out in *La señorita de Trevélez* is more interesting than the play's well-worn thesis. It is a genuine tragicomedy of a very Spanish kind: not a tragedy with comic interludes, but a drama where the main characters inspire pity while behaving in a thoroughly ridiculous way. In this respect, too, Arniches anticipates the *esperpento*, for whatever Valle-Inclán's stated intentions, there are moments when even the grotesque predicament of a Don Friolera is undeniably tragic. Like Friolera, Gonzalo de Trevélez is mortified above all by the absurdity of his situation, trapped in a tragic farce whose tragedy derives from his awareness of how farcical his predicament is. Arniches, however, did not develop the promise of seriousness beyond this point. Later works with titles like *¡Mecachis, qué guapo soy!* (1926) indicate that he had no real wish to become a Spanish

Ibsen, but preferred to go on giving the public lightweight entertainment. That the public's appetite for such entertainment was inexhaustible was demonstrated by the much greater depths of vulgarity,
plumbed by the immensely successful Pedro Muñoz Seca (1881-
1936), whose *astracanadas,* as the lowest form of the *género chico*
was called, with their coarse panderings to bourgeois philistinism
and right-wing political propaganda, are best forgotten.

The popularity of the conventional drama so far considered set up
barriers of public taste which shut writers of greater originality out
of the theatre. One result of this demoralising state of affairs was
to make some of them write plays which are frankly difficult to
stage or unsuitable for stage production, thus aggravating the
original problem. The matter of whether Valle-Inclán's dialogue
works should be considered as novels or drama has already been
mentioned, and is a case in point. The problem clearly stems from
the frustration of his attempts to bring something genuinely new to
the Spanish stage.

In his early years, Valle-Inclán wrote some plays which have a
better claim to be called *teatro poético* than anything by Marquina
or Pemán. One of his earliest theatrical ventures was an adaptation
of *Sonata de otoño,* entitled *El marqués de Bradomín,* staged without
much success in Madrid in 1906. The two *Comedias bárbaras* published in 1907 seemed to suggest that he was no longer interested in
the possibilities of *modernista* drama, but this proved not to be the
case. In 1909 he presented two plays in the theatre, *Cuento de abril,*
his first play in verse, and *La cabeza del dragón.* The use to which he
puts *modernista* material is different in the two plays. *Cuento de
abril* is prefaced by a poetic statement of intent which begins: 'La
divina puerta dorada / del jardín azul del ensueño / os abre mi vara
encantada / para deciros un cuento abrileño . . .' The ensuing
fantasy is set in medieval Provence, and the azure garden is none
other than the stylised 'parque viejo' of the *modernistas,* with its
roses, murmuring fountains, and tree-lined avenues. The main story
is the highly literary one of an unhappy troubadour's love for an
exquisite princess, and is treated with all the languid delicacy that
such a theme demands. The intrusion into this fairy-tale world of a
gang of austere, uncouth Castilian warriors possibly justifies some
allegorical reading (civilised pagan Europe meets barbaric Catholic
Spain), and of course the play, like all Valle-Inclán's works which

affect an exaggerated aestheticism, has an irrepressible element of self-parody, but these are very subsidiary features. *Cuento de abril* is essentially a virtuoso piece, in which Valle-Inclán shows off his mastery of modernist mannerisms. *La cabeza del dragón*, on the other hand, although set in a mythical, chivalresque world of princesses, fairies, and dragons, is a farce—'farsa infantil' he mischievously called it when he incorporated it into *Tablado de marionetas para educación de príncipes* in 1926—and it is in prose. Its treatment of royal personages, Ministers, generals, and the like, clearly looks forward to his later satires, and distinguishes it more sharply than *Cuento de abril* from what was then understood by *teatro poético*. The same is true of *La marquesa Rosalinda* (1912); in spite of its stylised setting—another aristocratic French eighteenth-century garden—and characters from the *commedia dell'arte*, it is aptly subtitled 'farsa sentimental y grotesca'. Amid its ingenious mixture of ancient theatrical traditions and recent poetic fashions, a grotesque vision persistently reduces the characters to absurd puppets.

Valle-Inclán's other contribution to poetic theatre at this period was his 'tragedia pastoril', *Voces de gesta* (1912). Like his novels about the Carlist War, it is the product of his sincere interest in the Carlist cause at this time. It also reflects the same preoccupation with decadence that had appeared in the *Comedias bárbaras*. But in other respects it is an unusual work for Valle-Inclán to have written, and one of the least suited to his peculiar gifts. It is his only verse tragedy, and his only attempt to achieve an epic tone in the theatre —for the *Comedias bárbaras*, in spite of their larger-than-life characters, are still domestic dramas. Valle-Inclán never returned to verse tragedy. By now he must in any case have been seriously disappointed by his lack of success on the stage. Unlike some of his contemporaries whose plays also failed to please the public, Valle-Inclán was very much a man of the theatre. Until he lost his arm he did a good deal of acting. His wife was an actress, and to the end of his life he continued to be personally involved in the theatrical world. But even before the end of the first decade of the century his plays possessed many of the characteristics which have provoked the debate as to whether they can, or should, or were meant to be performed on the stage at all. The debate can be pursued at different levels, but the three really important difficulties are practical ones: the technical problems of staging some of the effects, the problem of how to preserve or reflect in a stage production long stage directions of equal if not superior literary merit to the actual dialogue, and the indecency (by normal theatrical standards) of much of Valle-Inclán's work. A glance at most of the longer *acotaciones* of any of his plays will illustrate all three difficulties. *La marquesa Rosalinda* and all his subsequent verse dramas have their stage directions (if they can still be so called) in verse, and although it is sometimes argued that they give actors a deeper sense of what is required than the usual curt instructions from the author, a stage version which omits them cuts out the heart of the written text. Critics who wax indignant over the way the Spanish theatre has neglected Valle-Inclán's plays do not lack justification; but at the same time it must be said that most of his *obras dialogadas* need highly imaginative adaptation if their real force is to come through in a stage production.

In the cases of Unamuno and Azorín it is even harder to see how their dramatic works could be made into a satisfying theatrical experience—as distinct from the experience of a reader who may pause for reflection, turn back to an earlier page, and above all put the book down now and again for a rest. Unamuno's plays, as might be expected, are merely dialogue versions of the themes of his novels and essays. Though he wanted them performed, as one more way of stirring people's minds, he made no concessions to the demands of a stage production or of a theatre audience, and his dramatic work is not so much experimental theatre as a dramatised version of the literary and intellectual experiments which Unamuno performed in his prose writing. Azorín's drama, on the other hand, was intended as a theatrical experiment. Nearly all of it was written between 1926 and 1930. Starting with mystifying frivolous works like *Old Spain* (1926) and *Brandy, mucho brandy* (1927), his aim was decidedly to shock the theatre into change. Azorín believed that his plays would be performed when those of well-known contemporaries were long forgotten. As with his novels, it is surprising how this surge of interest in writing perplexingly unorthodox and avant-garde literature occurred precisely at a time when Azorín's social and political outlook had ossified into a definitive conservatism. An Academician since 1925, Azorín was one of the very few intellectuals or artists to support Primo de Rivera's dictatorship. Yet his sudden incursion into the theatre provoked consternation and scandal. Posterity has not yet confirmed his prediction that his plays would eventually win acclaim on the stage. His best theatre—*Lo invisible* (1927), made up of a prologue and three one-act plays, and *Angelita*

(1930)—is decidedly interesting, but in purely theatrical terms its merit is hard to assess. These plays are slow, anguished meditations on themes of death, time, and happiness, where symbolic characters perform symbolic actions in the same dream atmosphere of Azorín's novels of the period. There are no technical reasons why they should not be performed on the stage, but, like Unamuno's dramas, there is no reason why they should be acted. They have nothing to gain and much to lose from being exposed to the glare of the footlights in a commercial theatre.

The same accusation cannot be made, however, of the work of Jacinto Grau (1877-1958), who was a thoroughly professional dramatist, and had the melancholy satisfaction of seeing some of his plays succeed abroad when they had failed or had been rejected by the Spanish theatre. Although Grau varied his dramatic style and purpose over the years as a matter of principle, all his work is the result of a determination to rescue Spanish drama from its bourgeois triviality. Grau was a rather vain, cantankerous personality, and his lack of success in Spain deepened his not unreasonable conviction that only dramatists like himself could redeem the Spanish theatre. In his early works—*Entre llamas* (1915) and *El Conde Alarcos* (1917) —he responded, as did Unamuno, to the need to restore to drama the dimension of tragic grandeur and passion which Benavente and his school scrupulously avoided. Although Grau's early work is in prose, it is an elevated and stylised prose, more poetic than Marquina's verses. This remains true of his next play, *El hijo pródigo* (1918), a long, slow-moving work of great power. It begins by giving dramatic form to the biblical parable, but goes on to work in other elements: a stepmother's fatal passion for her stepson, a vivid evocation of rural life in biblical times, and an intensely dramatic conflict between the personalities of the brilliant, effortlessly attractive prodigal and his unlovable, mean-minded elder brother, whose tortured resentment, burning like a slow fuse through the play, compels sympathy and understanding. Grau's next and most famous play, *El señor de Pigmalión* (1921), is a 'farsa tragicómica'. It combines various meanings, all of which give it the unmistakable stamp of the epoch in which it was written. A prologue introduces some angry satire of Spanish theatre-managers' terror of anything that smells of art. The body of the play, published in the same year as *Luces de Bohemia* and Pirandello's *Six Characters* (though long after *Niebla*), concerns itself with the relation between an artist and the characters he invents, and with the theme of lifelike puppets and puppet-like humans. Pigmalión, as well as being Pygmalion, is another 'new Prometheus'. His robots rebel, escape, and finally murder him to ensure their freedom. The murder is seen both from the point of view of the puppets, when it recalls some of the problems explored in *Niebla*—the possibility and the limits of human freedom from a preordained fate, a creator's dependence on his creations—and from the point of view of Pigmalión himself, who dies reflecting on the 'triste sino del hombre héroe, humillado constantemente hasta ahora, en su soberbia, por los propios fantoches de su fantasía'—a statement which invites multiple interpretations, but which clearly expresses a twentieth-century pessimism about the dire condition into which man's ingenuity has led him. *El señor de Pigmalión* is a much more intellectual play than any of Grau's previous work, and such tragedy as it contains is the conceptualised tragedy of the absurd. This conceptualising tendency was pursued in his last works, notably when he returned, in *El burlador que no se burla* (1930), to the Don Juan theme which he had already treated in *Don Juan de Carillana* (1913). The later play is an interesting attempt to resume Don Juan's entire life-history and to probe the essence of his character in a succession of disconnected scenes—aspects of Don Juan, as it were. It is a highly intelligent, abstract play, which has never been staged.

If Grau had written his major works some years later, they might have stood a better chance of being staged successfully in Spain. During the Republic, the gathering impetus of a galaxy of fine writers in all literary genres, together with state encouragement of cultural experiment, threatened for a brief moment to invade the Spanish theatre and change its character. The prime mover in this achievement, as theatre audiences abroad know at least as well as those in Spain, was García Lorca. Lorca devoted serious attention to the theatre only in the last years of his short life. Up to about 1930 his forays into drama were mainly the result of youthful high spirits, celebrating with joyful frivolity the 'intranscendental' nature of art. An exception was his historical verse drama *Mariana Pineda* (1925), but it turned out to be exceptional in all respects. The young Lorca was an admirer of Marquina, and *Mariana Pineda* obviously owes much to this admiration, but Lorca appears to have regarded it as a mistake, for he never did anything in this style again. *La zapatera prodigiosa* (1930; written in 1926), though only a lightweight farce, is of some interest in its not altogether successful efforts to assure the audience that what they are watching is not a representation of marital problems in rural Andalusia, but a poetic fable of the human soul's pursuit of impossible dreams.[3] This is certainly Lorca's intention, but in spite of devices like characters without personal names, and the incorporation of song, dance, and pure nonsense, the play is rather realistic, and more similar to the Quintero brothers' Andalusian comedies than Lorca would have us believe. What he intends in *La zapatera* he achieves better in his short pieces of 1931, the 'aleluya erótica', *Amor de don Perlimplín con Belisa en su jardín*, and the 'farsa para guiñol', *Retablillo de don Cristóbal*. Also of 1931 is *Así que pasen cinco años*, which employs some disturbing, violent imagery not unlike that of *Poeta en Nueva York*. But up to this time Lorca was only playing with the theatre, and clearly treated it as one of the many marginal artistic interests, like music, painting, folklore, or lecturing, into which his poetic talents overflowed.

His more serious interest in drama dates from the early days of the Republic, and particularly from the setting-up of *La Barraca*, the theatrical company run mainly by students and unpaid amateurs, subsidised by the Ministry of Education, and whose principal function was to tour the country and bring to Spaniards who had never been in a theatre 'all the famous old plays which foreigners find so marvellous', as Lorca said in an interview in 1932. It was also about this time that Lorca began to make public statements about the profound importance to national life of a vigorous, popular theatre of good quality. These statements have given rise to discussion about the didactic intentions of his own later plays. The best-known remarks of this kind are in his *Charla sobre el teatro* of 1934, where he proclaims himself an 'ardiente apasionado del teatro de acción social', and calls the theatre

> uno de los más expresivos y útiles instrumentos para la edificación de un país . . . una tribuna libre donde los hombres pueden poner en evidenca morales viejas o equívocas y explicar con ejemplos vivos normas eternas del corazón y del sentimiento del hombre.[4]

But turning from these statements to Lorca's last four plays, it is not at once clear how the principles are meant to apply, or even what they mean. *Doña Rosita le soltera o el lenguaje de las flores* (1935), like the other three plays, is about frustrated womanhood, but it is set in a vanished and somewhat fantastic nineteenth-century world.

In the three rural tragedies, *Bodas de sangre* (1933), *Yerma* (1934), and *La casa de Bernarda Alba* (1936), such social moralising as can be extracted from the dramas is really quite conventional. We see that the subordination of instinct to social codes or material interests can have tragic consequences, that society denies women the sexual freedom it tolerates in men, and so on; but Lorca can hardly have meant to edify the nation with such commonplaces.

Clearly it was the theatre, not society, that Lorca wished to reform. When he wrote *La zapatera prodigiosa* in 1926, he said that his intention was to take a simple and realistic story, and turn it into a poetic myth. Although the tale itself was to be lifelike, he expressly wished to avoid giving the audience an illusion of reality.[5] This difficult combination is obviously also the aim of his tragedies. Lorca took the story of *Bodas de sangre* from a newspaper report; Bernarda Alba and her daughters were modelled on a real family he knew. Much of the language and some of the poetry of *Bodas de sangre* and *Yerma* were culled from the folklore of his native region. When foreigners imagine that Lorca's dramas faithfully represent Andalusian life, they may be, in the last resort, victims of a comical misconception, but the idea does not lack a certain basis in fact. However, Lorca's drama is nothing, as he vehemently affirmed,[6] if it does not succeed in turning life into literature.

It attempts to do this in a variety of ways. Ordinary villagers are transformed into archetypal figures, usually without personal names, personifying elemental attractions, revulsions, and incompatibilities which are not necessarily confined to Andalusia. The characters' natures, desires, and fears are expressed and emphasised by an elaborate apparatus of symbols: nowhere is this more evident than in *La casa de Bernarda Alba*, which Lorca introduces as having 'la intención de un documental fotográfico', but where in fact virtually everything—the white walls, the heat, the restless, stabled stallion, the metaphors of the dialogue, the fantasies of the mad grandmother —is invested with symbolic significance. Another way of making these harsh and basically sordid dramas poetic is simply by using poetry. Sometimes the verse passages are introduced realistically—in *Bernarda Alba* exclusively so—but even in these cases the song or lullaby that somebody sings is never a mere ornament, but always serves as a poetic gloss on the action, with symbolic significance that will emerge as the play proceeds. *Bodas de sangre* and *Yerma* also have sections of verse-dialogue, whose purpose is plainly to remind the audience of the difference between life and art. This is also partly the function of characters like the Moon and Death in *Bodas de sangre*, and the 'máscares populares' of *Yerma*, whom the children identify as the devil and his wife.

But another function of such allegorical characters is evidently to express a sense of tragic fate on which part of the force of the drama depends. In all three plays it might be observed that there are possible ways of avoiding the tragic dilemma: the Novia should not, for a start, marry the Novio; Yerma could have a child by another man; Bernarda's daughters could ignore the conventions of mourning and find husbands. But clearly the main theme of all the plays is that such sensible arrangements are precisely what the characters can never aspire to. The question then arises of what prevents them. In *Bodas de sangre* it is obviously something deeper than social convention, and something towards which Lorca has a highly ambivalent attitude. The Novio's mother predicts a fatal tragedy from the very first scene of the play. The Moon and Death wait impatiently but confidently for what amounts to the re-enactment of a tragic myth, and the deaths of Leonardo and the Novio are presented as ritual sacrifices in a poetic mystery of considerable beauty. Yet at the same time we are given to understand that the characters are also victims of a more prosaic and realistic determinism in the form of local conventions of honour, and, even more basically, of arranging marriages with an eye to material gain. The amalgam of myth and social realism, which was convincing in the poems of the *Romancero gitano*, is merely confusing in a play, and weakens its dramatic impact. Lorca appears to have realised this, but perhaps rather reluctantly. *Yerma* is more realistic. Until the last scene of the play, Yerma is simply trapped by her refusal to break the taboos of her tribe (though there are those in the tribe who urge her to do so). Yet the murder, if it is not to be regarded as sheer melodrama, once again suggests that she is acting out the dictates of dark, irrational forces. In *La casa de Bernarda Alba*, however, these mysterious forces have disappeared. Although Lorca still expresses his meaning in powerful and striking symbols, the meaning itself is entirely realistic and unmysterious.

Whether or not Lorca's drama could have revived the former glories of the Spanish theatre, as was his serious stated intention, if he had not died at the age of thirty-eight, is hard to say. The plays he wrote are experimental works which were still searching for the right formula and balance, as the difference between them shows.

Reading his plays affords the same kind of pleasure as reading his poetry: pleasure in the graceful ease with which he fuses traditional and popular elements with original and cultured ones, in his brilliant imagery which reaches deep into conscious and subconscious experience in what often seems an intuitive way, but is then thoughtfully organised into elegant artistic forms. These are poetic, rather than dramatic, gifts. *Yerma* would be a tedious play indeed if the obsessive reiteration of its theme were not embellished all the while by Lorca's poetic gifts, and the same is true of *Bernarda Alba*, in spite of its move in the direction of realism and its lack of verse dialogue.

Lorca's murder in 1936, however, as a prelude to the war, signalled the end, not only of his own, but of all such reforming aspirations. Since the war, Lorca's plays have been performed only rarely, Grau's never, whereas Benavente re-emerged as popular as ever. Political reasons have doubtless played their part. Benavente made some ferociously reactionary public statements after the war. Lorca, on the other hand, rightly or wrongly acquired a worldwide reputation as a martyr to left-wing principles. Grau ended his days in political exile. In this connection, the curious case of Alejandro Casona (1903-65), as Alejandro Rodríguez Álvarez called himself, is very revealing, and deserves consideration here, even though much of his work was done after the outbreak of the Civil War. Casona's early work—*La sirena varada* (1929; first performed 1934) and *Nuestra Natacha* (1936)— is made out of whimsical daydreams about a world which resembles the real one in some respects, but is improved by Casona's fantasy and becomes a better place to live in. *Nuestra Natacha* can also be interpreted as intending some mild criticism of bourgeois society. These plays were well received in the theatre. Casona, however, was a staunch supporter of the Republic, and the end of the war found him in exile in Argentina, where he continued to write successfully for the stage. *Prohibido suicidarse en primavera* (1937), *La dama del Alba* (1944), *La barca sin pescador* (1945), and *Los árboles mueren de pie* (1949) are his best-known works. They are by no means great plays. Although they often come to the verge of probing thoughtfully into serious matters, and adopt what promises to be effective dramatic techniques, they invariably fail to fulfil the promise, and veer off into whimsy. It is as if Casona did not grasp the point of the plays he was writing, and so failed to make anything worthwhile out of the Unamuno-like problems of identity and authenticity in *Prohibido suicidarse* and *Los árboles,* or the Lorca-like symbolic and archetypal characters of *La dama del alba.* But from the point of view of literary history, the quality of Casona's drama is less interesting than its reception in Spanish theatres. Official post-war Spain execrated the memory of Casona, enemy of the state. A reading of *Los árboles* by students of Barcelona University in 1951 provoked furious indignation in the Spanish press. But in 1962 Casona wearied of his exile, publicly repented the error of his ways, and returned to Spain. His works at once became gems of the modern Spanish theatre. As soon as he returned, *La dama del alba* had an extremely successful run in Madrid, and Casona's personal appearance on stage at the end of each performance was greeted with prolonged and evidently sincere applause.

Such a rapid and radical change of fortune invites reflection on what might not have been achieved by the dramatists of Lorca's generation if political strife had not interrupted their efforts to reform the Spanish theatre. Casona's drama, whatever its limitations, is not exactly in the tradition of the *alta comedia,* yet it has been well received by a public satisfied that it contains no offensive political material. In view of this there seems no real reason why the much more stimulating drama of Rafael Alberti should not one day be accorded the recognition it deserves in Spain. Alberti has not relented in his opposition to the present Spanish government, but most of his plays are not political, and they are more entertaining than much of the avant-garde theatre of his European contemporaries. Alberti and Lorca are alike as dramatists in several ways. Alberti was already a mature and established poet when he turned his attention seriously to the theatre in the early days of the Republic. Like Lorca, he saw an urgent need to reform it. In the *Hernani*-like tumult of the first performance of his first play, he is reported to have shouted '¡Abajo la podredumbre de la actual escena española!' He consciously sought inspiration for reform in the great drama of the Golden Age, but much of his material is also of popular or realistic origin. *Fermín Galán* (1931) is a series of *romances de ciego* in popular language about a real event from recent history. *El adefesio* (1944), like *Bernarda Alba,* is based on observation of an Andalusian family. *El trébol florido* (1940) and *La Gallarda* (1944) have rustic Spanish settings, and employ traditional folk-song in deliberate imitation of Lope de Vega's plays. Like Lorca, Alberti then transforms all this into highly original works of theatrical art, which invariably depend for their dramatic force on the presence of an inescapable tragic fate. This is particularly prominent in Alberti's first and in some ways most interesting play, *El hombre deshabitado*, first performed in 1931. It is an allegorical *auto* in the Calderonian manner, though ideologically it is the reverse of an *auto sacramental*. It treats the theme of original sin and paradise lost in a modern fashion. A shadowy, inscrutable divinity, 'El Vigilante Nocturno', presides over the encounter of 'El Hombre' and 'La Mujer' with 'La Tentación', accompanied by a Chorus of the Five Senses, and ends by condemning Man to a perpetual Hell. The ancient myth of the Fallen Angel is reworked into a modern theology of a senselessly evil divinity and a helplessly doomed mankind locked together in eternal mutual hatred, 'Te aborreceré siempre', cries El Hombre at the last. 'Y yo a tí, por toda la eternidad', replies El Vigilante Nocturno, an absurd and sinister god, who proclaims his nature in his final revelation that 'mis juicios son un abismo profundo'. *El hombre deshabitado* is an imposing, disturbing creation, spun in part from the fearful imagery of *Sobre los ángeles*, and reflecting the awful sense of inner void which afflicted Alberti and Lorca in the late twenties. But it ran for a month on the Madrid stage. *Fermín Galán*, on the other hand, caused such a furore that the safety curtain had to be lowered to protect the actors from the public. But this second work was calculated to arouse political passions. Alberti commented sarcastically that his mistake had been to show it to a bourgeois public instead of peasants, but this was a political comment, not an artistic one. The considerable success of *El hombre deshabitado* with the bourgeois public suggests that Alberti and Lorca were beginning to have some effect on public taste.

When that effect was nipped in the bud by the war, Alberti continued to write highly imaginative plays which have been staged with due acclaim abroad. The best of them is *El adefesio*, which transforms a sordid little tale of provincial frustration and hypocrisy into an eminently theatrical mixture of horror, absurdity, tragedy, and farce. If the play can be described as surrealistic, it is only in the controlled sense that it throws a lurid light down dark corridors of the subconscious minds of the characters. The fatal determinism which governs *El adefesio* may appear to have a more realistic explanation than in *El hombre deshabitado*, for the all-powerful Gorgo knows that the youngsters whose marriage she prevents are children of the same father, her own brother. But the reasonableness of this explanation is quite submerged in Alberti's treatment of

Gorgo's weird cult of the memory of her dead brother, whose beard she wears to enhance her authority, and whose name she invokes in ritual religious fashion (sometimes confusing it with that of God) to justify the torture of her niece and to account for her part in her niece's suicide. The occasional verse passages of *El adefesio*, although they sometimes intensify the poignancy of Altea's doomed love, are used mostly to make Gorgo's incantations more macabre than ever. But in the rural dramas, *El trébol florido* and *La Gallarda*, Alberti employs more of the popular lyrical elements out of which some of his earlier poetry was made. The latter work is entirely in verse. But both plays are even further from being picturesque sketches of Andalusian life than are Lorca's tragedies. Alberti creates poetic myths on themes of love, death, and fate. Characters with strange, evocative names (sometimes, like Gorgo's, suggesting Classical antecedents) assume archetypal stature. The figure which dominates *La Gallarda*, though never seen, is a fighting bull which La Gallarda regards as both child and lover, and which kills her husband. Her intensely passionate devotion to the animal is of a distinctly mystical kind, and raises many legendary echoes. Inescapable tragedy awaits the characters from the start. In the prologue, the mysterious Babú, who acts as Chorus, assures us that we must resign ourselves to our destiny, for we can do nothing to change it. These are spectacular, powerful plays of great formal beauty and poetic elegance. They stimulate the imagination and set it moving among paths of its own —sometimes by baffling it, it is true, but never gratuitously so. Although they are dramas that repay careful, unhurried reflection, it is easy to see when reading them that their immediate effect on a theatre audience would be exciting. They are not merely the by-products of a fine poet, but excellent plays in their own right, which deserve to be better known.

A third writer who turned to the theatre after he had established his reputation as a poet was Miguel Hernández. Like other experimental dramatists of the period, he wished to break with current theatrical conventions by restoring to Spanish drama some of its traditional features, particularly those of his beloved Golden Age. In his youthful, Catholic period, he had attempted a modern *auto sacramental*, *Quien te ha visto y quien te ve* (1933). But his conversion to Communism produced one notable contribution to the modern theatre before Hernández's untimely death, *El labrador de más aire* (1937). Like *El trébol florido*, this play looks to Lope de Vega for its timeless rural Spanish setting, the lyrical grace of its fluent *décimas*, and its theme of social justice. But it also has a modern polemical intent. Juan, the 'labrador de más aire' of the village, eloquently inveighs against his fellow-peasants' age-old custom of resigning themselves to exploitation, and of seeking cowardly consolation in the tavern instead of raising 'una hoz de rebeldía/y un martillo de protesta' against capitalist landowners. The latter win in the end; Juan is basely murdered for his insolence in trying to rise from the condition of a farm animal to a state of human dignity. A tender elegy from his beloved softens the crudity of the thesis, and delicately draws together the various strands of this unusual, elegantly simple, verse-play.

The one remaining dramatist of the period whose work might conceivably interest future generations is Enrique Jardiel Poncela (1901-52). His drama really belongs to all four categories considered in this chapter—bourgeois-realist, poetic, *costumbrista*, and experimental. Some of it is in verse, some in prose. *Angelina o el honor de un brigadier* (1933) is a pastiche of late nineteenth-century drama. Jardiel himself seems to have believed that his most characteristic type of comedy, starting in 1927 with *Una noche de primavera sin sueño* and continuing until well after the Civil War, was experimental work which contributed to the revitalisation of the theatre. His best play is *Eloisa está debajo de un almendro* (1940), an entertaining, professionally competent piece which seeks to combine comically realistic dialogue (notably in the long *costumbrista* 'prologue' in a Madrid cinema) with absurd fantasy. But the fantasy turns out to be mere situation comedy. Intricate skeins of madness in the first act, which might appear to be involving the audience in a world as disturbing as that of *El adefesio*—were it not for the presence of a pair of servants who are also baffled by what is going on—are all unravelled at the end, in the manner of a detective novel, so that everything has its logical explanation and it has all been a matter of misunderstanding. In fact Jardiel Poncela's plays represent a curious attempt on the part of traditional bourgeois comedy to come to some sort of arrangement with certain experimental tendencies in the modern theatre. But it misses, or avoids, the point of what is normally understood by the Theatre of the Absurd, and in the end repeats what was by 1940 a very old-fashioned message: that however perplexing life may seem, there is a reasonable explanation for everything, and so there is no need to worry.

NOTES

1. See G. Torrente Ballester, *Teatro español contemporáneo* (2nd edn., Madrid, 1968), pp. 94-8.

2. J. Ortega y Gasset, *Obras completas* (Madrid, 1946-), I, 106.

3. See F. García Lorca, *Obras completas* (4th edn., Madrid, 1960), pp. 1694-5.

4. Ibid., pp. 33-6.

5. Ibid., pp. 1695-6.

6. Ibid., p. 1717.

7. An important new study by R. Martínez Nadal, *El público. Amor, teatro y caballos en la obra de F. García Lorca* (Oxford, 1970) makes it clear that Lorca's play *El público*, a draft of which Sr. Nadal possesses, is an extremely original and unconventional work which, if it had been published or performed during Lorca's lifetime, might have been a most important contribution to Spanish drama.

Chapter 4

LITERATURE SINCE THE CIVIL WAR

I. THE NOVEL IN EXILE

A POET MAY WELL HAVE COMPLETED HIS BEST WORK by the time he is forty. It is much rarer for a novelist to have done so. When the brilliant generation of poets considered in Chapter 2 was dispersed by the war, they had already written the poetry on which their reputations rest. With the exception of Cernuda, it is fair to regard their post-war work as a mere postscript to what they had produced in the twenties and thirties. Furthermore, although they formed no school nor followed any single principle, they were a group of friends, united and stimulated by mutual respect and common enthusiasm for their art. Novelists of the same age as these poets, however, formed no such group. In exile they have followed separate paths, and the best of them have produced more impressive work since 1939 than anything they had written before leaving Spain.

A singular and extreme instance of this is provided by Arturo Barea (1897-1957), who had only written a few short stories before 1939, but whose trilogy *La forja de un rebelde*, which originally appeared in English (1941-44), suddenly transformed him into the most famous living Spanish novelist. The trilogy foreshadowed several things to come. Its world-wide success was largely due to its account of the Civil War, although only the third volume, *La llama*, deals with this period, and Barea saw the war from an office in Madrid. The other two parts reach back into the author's early life and his experience as a soldier in the Moroccan War, and provide both a personal testimony of what made Barea a socialist and an impression of the grass-root origins of the national cataclysm. The book is entirely devoid of artifice, carelessly written, uneven in structure and tempo. Strictly speaking it is not a novel at all, but only Barea's memories of what he saw and felt and thought. People and places are given their real names, and though Barea proclaims his total commitment to partisan principles, actual events are related with considerable impartiality. The result is a document of absorbing social and historical interest, whose only creative element is Barea's blunt, unpolished style. Thousands of Spaniards could have told similar stories, and several have actually done so, but few with the power and vividness of Barea's narrative manner, which, particularly in the first volume of the trilogy, inescapably invites comparison with Baroja's. To a limited extent the immediacy and economy of his portrayal of reality redeems his other novel, *La raíz rota* (1952). This time it is a real fiction, for the protagonist returns to Spain from exile in London, as Barea never did. In this disappointing book, with its sadly mistaken vision of what post-war Spain must be like, Barea reveals that his literary talent was his capacity for recording faithfully and forcibly his own real experience.

Whereas Barea was a writer with just one fine book in him, the vast production in every conceivable literary genre of Max Aub (1903-) makes it impossible to classify him or summarise his work succinctly. His writing before the war shows him to have been faithful to the principle that art is an ingenious game which may distract us from a drab reality. Since the war, in exile in Mexico, Aub's enormous literary energy—which shows no sign of flagging as he approaches his seventies—has produced a torrent of plays, stories, novels, and essays on a rich variety of themes. But as a novelist, his central achievement is his great cycle of books about the Civil War, beginning with *Campo cerrado* (1943; dated 1939) and ending with *Campo de los almendros* (1968), collectively entitled *El laberinto mágico*. Although the cycle, like *La forja de un rebelde*, begins some years before the war, and in its own way seeks to explain the origins and significance of the conflict, nothing could be less like Barea's plain and personal narrative. Aub is more concerned with analysis and interpretation than with a record of events, and the result is a major work of art which involves the reader emotionally in Aub's vision of the conflagration. A fragmented technique of short passages —conversations, encounters, flashbacks, anecdotes—weaves the stories of many hundreds of characters into a dense and varied tapestry. Some of the characters appear briefly in a single scene or anecdote; others occupy the foreground for long periods; a few reappear repeatedly throughout the series, so that we come to know them well. Some are historical, some fictional, but most are both, for as Aub says in a direct authorial intervention in *Campo de los almendros,* as far as his memories and his novels are concerned, the difference between real people and characters who have lived beside them in his imagination during the thirty years he has devoted to the cycle is a meaningless one. Moreover, the novels have no protagonists. The characters who appear most frequently are simply the ones whom Aub chooses to observe most closely as representative of attitudes and mentalities which offer insights into what the war was about.

The greater part of the series takes the form of conversation, which Aub handles with complete authority, whether it is a matter of a furious exchange of obscenities or an intricate philosophical discussion among intellectuals. The talk ranges over a wide variety of topics, but the main one is the war, what caused it, why it is being fought, and ultimately, why it was lost, and when, and by whom. But Aub has more than a keen ear for other people's talk. His own linguistic resources are extremely rich and varied. *El laberinto mágico* is not only indispensable reading for anyone who wants to fathom the psychological origins of the Spanish Civil War; it is also indisputably the most impressive work of literary art among the host of novels produced by the war.

El laberinto mágico is the finest achievement in Aub's immense literary output, but its fame has been at least temporarily eclipsed by that of *Jusep Torres Campalans* (1958). This is the biography and study of a Catalan painter, friend and contemporary of Picasso, and an important figure in the artistic revolution of the early years of the century, whose indifference to glory and eventual abandonment of painting in order to go and live among Mexican Indians have caused him to be completely forgotten today. It is an absorbing book, with detailed documentation, reproductions of some of the paintings, and serious reflections on art. But in spite of a photograph of Torres Campalans and Picasso together, it is wholly the product of Aub's own imagination and ingenuity. There was never any such painter. The book naturally led many people to believe that he had existed, and even, it is said, elicited reminiscences from some who claimed to have known him; but it is more than an elaborate hoax. In the first place it presents an extremely interesting account of the psychology of an unusual artist. Then its serious meditations on the function of art—which are not confined to painting—provide some indication of why Aub chose to write the book as a biographical study. If a Torres Campalans had really existed, his biography would still be a book, a work of literature, which is something quite different from the life of a man. The point is relevant to Aub's methods, and his interpolated comments, in the novels of *El laberinto mágico*: as many writers have realised since Aristotle, if a fiction contains a human truth, it may matter little whether or not the characters who embody it *also* lived real lives in the real world.

Another novelist in exile whose extensive production—some forty novels to date—shows no sign of abating with age is Ramón J. Sender (1902-   ). In such a large and varied output, one can only call attention to the principal themes of his work and the way in which they are treated. Most of his early writing is on socio-political subjects. As a young man, Sender held extreme left-wing political views, which are reflected in such works as *O.P.* (1931), *Siete domingos rojos* (1932), and the semi-documentary *Viaje a la aldea del crimen* (1934). *Mr. Witt en el Cantón* (1935), which won him Spain's national prize for literature, is set in 1873, during the first Spanish republic, but in 1935 much of its matter was once again topical and even prophetic. A visit to Russia in 1933 made Sender sceptical of Stalinist Communism, and his scepticism deepened into bitter antipathy during the war, when, as a fighting soldier, he came to regard the Party's role in the struggle as disastrous for Spain. After 1939 Sender's own experience of pre-war and wartime Spain continued to provide material for his novels, notably for the three weighty volumes of *Crónica del alba* (1942-66) and for *Los cinco libros de Ariadna* (1957). The manner of all these books is mainly realistic, though not consistently so, and even in the midst of apparently conventional realistic narrative, Sender's readers must expect to be frequently disconcerted by both strange ideas and unusual methods of presentation. A typical example is the general structure of *Los cinco libros de Ariadne*, where a fairly straightforward narrative of two people's experience of the Civil War is set in a framework of weird fantasy. The fantasy is clearly symbolic—some of the allusions are plain enough for it to be certain that this is so; but precisely what the many mysterious details of the fantasy symbolise is something that no commentator has yet managed to establish convincingly.

Sender's tendency towards mystery, in both matter and manner, becomes much more pronounced in his post-war novels. Although it makes parts of his writings frankly impenetrable, its purpose is quite serious. Sender is deeply interested in mysterious and secret things—myth, magic, ritual, legend—which resist rational explanation and upset conventional habits of thought. Like D. H. Lawrence, whose work he admires, Sender believes that to try to interpret the world and our place in it exclusively by means of logical and scientific analysis is to deny an important part of our humanity. Sender thinks that highly civilised modern societies, by cutting themselves off from their primitive roots, have unnecessarily restricted their access to certain truths which may be apprehended by means of intuitions and revelations which are essentially religious. Some readers will find such notions unpalatable, and will regard Sender's veritable obsession with historically persistent superstitions as either perplexing or simply naïve. But the fictions he has made out of these notions are often highly original and powerful assaults on the imagination. The dream-like world of *Epitalamio del Prieto Trinidad* (1942), populated by criminals and by the Indians who represent magical-religious wisdom in many of Sender's novels, the black magic and elaborate cosmic mythology of *Emen Hetan* (1958) and *Las criaturas saturnianas* (1968), the cryptic philological-mythological theories in many books, on such subjects as the mystical properties of words beginning with the letters Sp—, make for mystifying reading which can be tiresome and obscure at times, but more often testify to an immensely fertile and wide-ranging imagination, disposed to explore all kinds of curious and esoteric subjects in the hope that they will yield new insights into the nature of life.

The insights that Sender seeks are above all ethical ones. At the heart of his work is a preoccupation with the nature of good and evil, of moral responsibility, sin and guilt. A persistent idea of Sender's is that such problems can be seriously approached only by individuals whose response to moral issues has somehow been purged of petty irrelevances like fear, indignation, envy, or greed. The purging usually takes place as the result of some violent psychological shock, and produces a kind of superficial moral numbness, which is the out-ward sign of an inner detachment and serenity without which, says Sender, clear moral perceptions are impossible. The protagonists of *Le Esfera* (1947), *El verdugo afable* (1952), and *Las criaturas saturnianas* (1968)—perhaps his finest book to date—are outstanding examples of individuals whose circumstances have freed their imagi-nations in this way.

Sender's inquiry into fundamental ethics has been serious and pro-longed. His habit of incorporating ideas, events, whole sections from his earlier work in later novels is not due, in a writer of such prolific inventiveness, to his having nothing new to say, but precisely the opposite. He constantly rethinks, modifies, and develops his ideas. *Las criaturas saturnianas* is a greatly afplified and altered version of *Emen Hetan*. The 1947 edition of *La Esfera* was a new version of *Proverbio de la muerte*; further alterations were made in an English translation (*The Sphere*) of 1949, and a third Spanish edition of 1969, which Sender says is definitive, again makes changes. Sender's inquiry does not produce any certain conclusions. It is not his way to tell the reader what to believe, or even what he himself believes, but rather to open up the reader's imagination and set it working along paths of its own. In his best work he achieves this aim in a most stimulating manner. Sender's prefatory note to the latest edition of *La Esfera* sums up exactly and concisely the purpose of all his mature writing: 'El propósito de *La Esfera* es más iluminativo que constructivo, y trata de sugerir planos místicos en los que el lector pueda edificar sus propias estructuras'.

Although younger than Aub and Sender, Francisco Ayala (1906-) published his first book when he was eighteen, and soon became known for his contributions to the *Revista de Occidente* and for a steady production of stories culminating in *Cazador en el alba* (1930). His pre-war writing is characterised by a dedicated aestheticism subjected to a keen intelligence, and the result is fiction similar to that of Jarnés, of minimal anecdotal or descriptive interest, pursuing brilliant metaphor with tireless ingenuity. Such writing is out of fashion, and Ayala himself has spoken unkindly of his early work in retrospect. But *Cazador en el alba* is a very impressive achievement for a twenty-three-year-old. Ayala, however, spent 1929 and 1930 in the sinister atmosphere of the Berlin of those years. What he observed there, and in Spain and the rest of the world in the dark years that followed, changed his attitude to art sharply. His fiction struck him as frivolous, and he wrote no more of it for nearly twenty years, turning his talents instead to what remains an important part of his writing, essays and books on sociological, philosophical, and literary topics. Like most of his fellow-writers in exile, he has earned his living principally as a university teacher.

When he returned to creative fiction with *Los usurpadores* (1949), it was of a different kind from his pre-war work. The book consists of six stories on themes from Spanish history, followed by a 'Diálogo de los muertos' referring to the Civil War. Though there is no narrative continuity among the seven pieces, the title indicates their common theme. The 'usurpation' in question is that which always occurs, according to Ayala, when one man seeks to subjugate another to his will. Ayala treats this universal immorality from different points of view in finely written fables, writing now out of indignation and pessimism, but still with intelligence and artistry. The best story, 'El hechizado', adds deep irony to the book with its perspective of the colossal labyrinth of Spanish imperial authority, ruling the lives of millions of human beings in the name of the pathetic imbecile, Charles II, who drools uncomprehendingly at its centre. A second book of stories published in 1949, *La cabeza del cordero* (1949), also applies different points of view to a single subject, this time the Civil War. The four tales move from the psychological origins to the reality of the war, and from there to the matter of exile and the problems of returning. Once again the interest is analytic, not anecdotal, and the stories are parables which provoke serious thought.

A further book of short stories, *Historia de macacos* (1955), seemed to indicate that Ayala had decided to devote himself entirely to short narratives, but in 1958 he published a novel which is widely and justifiably regarded as the best book he has written so far, *Muertes de perro*. Although its tale of squalid brutality and human degradation is set in a Spanish-American republic which recalls both *Tirano Banderas* and Conrad's *Nostromo*, Ayala has said explicitly that his theme is not a local manifestation of evil, but 'el desamparo en que se vive hoy'.[1] *Muertes de perro* is another parable about the modern world as a whole, where people live like mindless beasts and die like dogs, obscurely and meaninglessly; it is notable that although the novel has to do with what in a different sort of world would be called affairs of state, none of the sordid series of murders and bestialities is the result of any principle or belief. Moreover, as the narrator ironically observes, and as a sequel to the novel, *El fondo del vaso* (1962), confirms, the tyranny of the swinish dictator Bocanegra, hateful and cruel as it was, gave the state its only possible sort of order, so that in the chaos following his murder people look back to his rule as to a Golden Age.

The way in which this grisly tale is presented, though not exactly original, is extremely accomplished, and adds an extra dimension of interest to what might otherwise sometimes become a mere catalogue of ugliness. The narrator says he plans to write an orderly and objective history of the events in due course. But we may be sure that such a history would be far less revealing—and less suitable to

Ayala's real purpose—than the collection of notes and documents which constitute *Muertes de perro,* and which offers a variety of perspectives, including the barbed commentaries of the narrator himself, who is as mean and vicious an individual as any of his compatriots. Moreover, the 'disorder' of the notes and documents allows Ayala to exploit sophisticated fictional techniques in a natural way which runs no risk either of obscurity or of straining after artificial effects. Liberated from a strict chronological order of events, the narrative can contain anticipation of the future, pondering on the past, and, above all, the excitement generated by the classic device of 'withheld truth'. We know, for example, from an early stage in the novel that Tadeo Requena is going to murder Bocanegra, but until nearly the end we do not know how or why. In a similar way, the appearance in the narrator's notes of incidents which he thinks will be of little importance to his definitive account of the events permits Ayala to make unobtrusive use of their symbolic significance —notably in respect of the various dogs who live and die in the pages of *Muertes de perro.*

Ayala, like Sender and Aub, is alive and well, living mainly in the United States, and still writing books which are at last becoming available to a Spanish public. Until very recent years, the writings of these important Spanish novelists—to whose names a less limited account would add those of Rosa Chacel (1896-), Segundo Serrano Poncela (1912-), Manuel Andújar (1913-), and the famous essayist, historian, and diplomat Salvador de Madariaga (1886-) who has lived in England since the Civil War—have been almost unknown in Spain. But the situation is changing rapidly. It is now legitimate at least to hope that the hitherto necessary division of Spanish literature since the war into literature in Spain and literature in exile is coming to an end, and that increasing familiarity with the work of illustrious Spanish writers outside Spain may interest and encourage novelists inside Spain to overcome the problems which have beset them since 1939.

II. LITERATURE IN SPAIN

The years immediately following the Civil War were, for most Spaniards, almost as grim as the war years themselves. For many they meant extreme poverty and hunger among the ruins of a ravaged land. The victors of the war were in no mood to forgive and forget, and the numbers of Spain's widows and orphans were further swollen by executions and imprisonment. The new regime of law and order meant only harsh suppression of potential subversion, and the government remained unable or unwilling to tackle either the problems of the aftermath of war or the cynical exploitation of national disaster by opportunists. At the end of the World War, most foreign countries ostracised Spain for her association with the Axis powers and her illiberal regime. As well as aggravating the desperate economic situation, this created a siege mentality which was in every way unpropitious for the arts. Since most writers and artists had supported the Republican cause, and had departed into exile after the war, the minions of the new regime regarded those that remained with great suspicion. Censorship was severe and arbitrary, though often not severe enough for the press, or for private citizens quick to call public attention to the slightest deviation from the principles for which the Catholic, bourgeois Right had fought and won a bloody war. Censorship of foreign writing was equally tight, and it was difficult and even dangerous for young writers to find out what was going on abroad, or what was being written by their exiled compatriots. There was therefore a sharp break in literary continuity. Unamuno, Valle-Inclán, Antonio Machado, and Lorca were dead, the great majority of the best writers had disappeared, and those who stayed or returned were mere ghosts of their former selves. In a stifling and generally hostile atmosphere, preoccupied by the misery and injustice that surrounded them, Spanish writers had to make hesitant new beginnings under the watchful eye of an all-powerful censorship. The forties were understandably lean years for Spanish literature.

The fifties, however, saw certain changes in Spain's national and international situation. With the Cold War at its coldest, the Western democracies took note of Spain's vociferous anti-Communism. The decision to exclude Spain from the United Nations until her dictatorship was replaced with a more liberal regime was revoked in 1950, and in 1955 she was admitted unconditionally, with an unchanged regime, to the General Assembly. In 1951 the United States began to negotiate an agreement to establish military bases in Spain in exchange for substantial economic aid. Tourism and foreign investment began to help the economy. And as the regime's isolationist mood gradually relaxed, the atmosphere inside Spain began to change. Franco, who had refused to make any concessions to liberalism when asked to do so by foreign powers, now began to seek a more benevolent image. The small improvements resulting from these changes in the middle fifties had the effect, as is often the case, of awakening active discontent. After fifteen years Spaniards were beginning to lose their fear—so diligently exploited by the regime— that any opposition to authority would start another civil war.

Active protest against economic and social injustice has come from various sections of Spanish society during the last two decades; there have been industrial strikes, student demonstrations, separatist move- ments in Catalonia and the Basque provinces, and, increasingly, con- demnation of the regime by the clergy. Much of the best literature of the post-war period belongs to this ferment of protest. Novelists, dramatists, and poets of the fifties and sixties have conceived their task as one of bearing witness to an intolerable reality, or speaking the truth in a world of lies, evasions, silences. The result has been a largely introspective literature of social realism, of consider- able importance to the student of the social history of post-war Spain, but very limited in its appeal to a wider audience. Proximity in time can produce large errors of perspective, and such evaluations as are offered in this chapter are intended as extremely tentative; but it is safe to say that the post-war period in Spain has produced no litera- ture which remotely approaches the quality of the best work of the twenties and thirties. Rightly or wrongly—and those who have not spent the last thirty years in Spain are in no position to lay down priorities—Spanish literature during this period has been concerned with testimony rather than invention. There have been many sincere and serious writers, but no great or original ones. The literary history of this age is therefore perhaps best presented as an account of tendencies, rather than of outstanding works of art. If literary excel- lence is adopted as a criterion of importance, the account must also be brief compared with that of the earlier part of the century. Other criteria may of course be applied, and those who regard contemporary literature as important because it is contemporary will find the following pages inadequate.

III. THE NOVEL

The most interesting novel published in Spain during the decade after the Civil War was *La familia de Pascual Duarte* (1942) by

Camilo José Cela (1916-). The so-called *tremendismo* of this shocking, repulsive tale has contributed much to its fame, but it is far from being its most impressive feature. In fact the novel's chief merit is its subtlety, in its revelation that the violent peasant protagonist, outwardly brutalised by a fatal chain of circumstances, is a tragically complicated personality, struggling with the intolerable psychological burdens of a genuine sensitivity, a demanding and potentially noble moral conscience, and a manifestly Oedipal relationship with his odious mother—whom he murders, as the attentive reader will observe, in the same passionately ambivalent mood as that of his first violent act of love with his wife. To have conveyed all this through the challenging medium of the personal reminiscences of an untutored villager, is a very considerable literary achievement. But it turned out to be a somewhat isolated one, both in respect of Cela's writing and of Spanish fiction in general. Cela has been one of the very few truly experimental novelists in post-war Spain, and no two of his books are alike. After *La familia de Pascual Duarte* he wrote *Pabellón de reposo* (1944), an ingeniously structured account of the subjective states of seven patients dying from tuberculosis in a sanatorium. Cela's third book was *Nuevas andanzas de Lazarillo de Tormes* (1944), which relates the experiences of a twentieth-century *pícaro*. It is extremely well written, but hardly the great book one might have expected from the youthful author of *Pascual Duarte*. For five years after this Cela wrote no more novels.

Other novelists of the forties and fifties returned to the business of trying to interest a wide public. In this they were encouraged by the institution of numerous literary prizes awarded by publishing houses with one eye on prestige and the other on sales. The public's appetite for a good read was currently being competently catered to by the old-fashioned, conventional realism of writers like J. A. Zunzunegui (1902-), I. Agustí (1913-), and, in the fifties, A. M. de Lera (1912-), and the awarders of prizes clearly took note of their success. The first Premio Nadal of 1944 went to *Nada*, by Carmen Laforet (1921-), and showed the shape of things to come. Realism had returned with a vengeance, effacing all memory of the novelistic experiments of the twenties. *Nada* is simply a slice of the life of a young university student, and records faithfully, in a first person narrative, what happens to her during one year spent in the sordid, grey world of post-war Barcelona. As an exercise in re-creating an unpleasant reality in words it is well done, but that is its only aim and achievement.

6 * *

In general, the Nadal prizewinners of the forties, including Carmen Laforet, have not fulfilled whatever promise the juries thought they saw in their works. Two exceptions, of rather different kinds, are José Gironella (1917-   ) and Miguel Delibes (1920-   ). Gironella is known less for *El hombre* (1947), which won him the prize, than for his vast trilogy about the Civil War: *Los cipreses creen en Dios* (1953), *Un millón de muertos* (1961), and *Ha estallado la paz* (1966). It is probable that no novels have been more widely read in Spain since the war. The questions of their objectivity and literary merit have given rise to heated controversy, in which Gironella has taken a lively part, and which has made him an aggressive champion of the view that there is no shame in writing novels which appeal to a huge public. Since the first volume of the trilogy appeared, it has become clear that Gironella's formula of appearing to give the Republican case a fair hearing without ultimately offending *franquista* sentiments appeals strongly to many Spanish readers. A more recent product in this rich vein is Lera's immensely successful *Las últimas banderas* (1967).

As regards appealing to a large public, Miguel Delibes, as is his way in all things, has taken a middle course. Since he won the 1947 Nadal prize with *La sombra del ciprés es alargada*, his steady output of novels has won him general esteem, but he has not set out to court popular favour, and his books assert certain principles and values which are not, according to Delibes, generally recognised by Spanish society. The positive aspect of these principles shows in his concern for simple and natural things as a relief from the ugliness and complexity of modern life. Delibes is determinedly and contentedly provincial, and his sunniest books, such as *El camino* (1950), *Diario de un cazador* (1955), *Las ratas* (1962), are pleasantly unsentimental stories of children and country life, written in a strong, clear style which makes them immediately attractive. No reader, however fond of the novels, is likely to think Delibes a great novelist, but his mediocrity is of an honest and dignified kind which commands respect. The same may be said of the ideological content of his novels. Delibes is a serious, if moderate, critic of his society, a committed liberal Catholic who finds a deplorable lack of true Christianity in Spain. His targets are those of any decent man: hypocrisy, intolerance, selfishness, and greed. A recent novel, *Cinco horas con Mario* (1966), catalogues them in detail, in nearly three hundred pages of interior monologue from the unrelievedly disagreeable mind of Mario's widow.

Nobody could find Delibes's mild-mannered appeal to decency either objectionable or subversive. The novel of the fifties, however, saw the appearance of a sterner school of social criticism. Its precursor was Cela, who has always, for whatever reason, been able to get away with things which the censor would not permit in other writers. In 1948 he had published *Viaje a la Alcarria*, a finely written travelogue through one of the poorest and most backward areas of Spain. His novel *La colmena* (1951) shifts the scene to Madrid, and presents a microscopically detailed sample of the wretchedness of life in the capital. The way in which Cela employs subtle artistic devices in order to convey an impression of documentary realism is exceedingly skilful, and *La colmena* has had a considerable impact on younger writers. What attracted these writers was, however, more the matter than the manner of Cela's novel. *La colmena* is technically ambitious. Multiple perspectives bring depth as well as detail to the account of two ordinary days in the lives of nearly three hundred characters; chronology is broken up for analytical and aesthetic effect, and there is no plot in the normal sense of the word, indeed a final section of the novel seems to stress the impossibility of explaining clear chains of cause and effect. In comparison with Cela's restless probings into the different possible relationships between art and reality, the younger novelists adopted very conventional narrative techniques. The lead that Cela gave them was in taking as his theme the bitter reality of life in post-war Spain, a hungry, suffering, cynical, brutalised world. After *La colmena* there occurred a sudden flowering (in spite of the censor's energetic prunings) of young literary talent dedicated to the cause of exposing, or at least testifying to, the miseries of Spanish life, and expressing itself in the stark, objectively realistic manner which the subject seemed to demand. A large number of serious, well-written novels of this kind in the fifties seemed to promise much for the future. Their subject was invariably the somewhat limited one of contemporary Spain, and for the most part the novels were technically unadventurous; but the conscientious testimony of these writers, most of whom were only children during the Civil War, but had now reached an age when they were able to assess its effects with an honesty they found absent from the national press and radio, came like a breath of fresh air to Spanish letters. A complete list of the writers who contributed to this minor renaissance of the Spanish novel would be very long, but it would certainly include the names of Ana María Matute, Sánchez Ferlosio, Juan and Luis

Goytisolo, Aldecoa, Fernández Santos, García Hortelano, Carmen Martín Gaite, López Pacheco, Sueiro, and Elena Quiroga.

Their concept of the novel as an instrument of protest naturally limited the universal appeal of the work of these writers, as many of them have realised. Juan Goytisolo has observed that the Spanish novel of the fifties and sixties assumed the informative and critical duties which in a free society would be performed by news services. Its content is therefore of interest only to those who are interested in contemporary Spain, which does not even mean all Spaniards: there are many, perhaps the majority, who do not wish to know the kind of thing these novelists tell them. They were therefore writing for a small group of readers—and fellow-writers—who shared their preoccupations and sympathised with their attitudes. Their urgent sense of duty as honest witnesses virtually bound them to the techniques of objective realism, at a time when exiled Spaniards and Spanish American writers were experimenting interestingly with alternative literary forms. The supreme monument to such realism, and an extremely influential novel in Spain, was Rafael Sánchez Ferlosio's *El Jarama* (1956). Yet if *El Jarama* is the best book to have been written by this group of writers, it is not because of its realism, but because of its symbolic depths and its subtle recourse to realms of mystery and poetry.[2] Superficially, its incredibly patient record of the pointless conversations of a host of uninteresting people makes it, no doubt intentionally, one of the most boring works in the history of the novel.

When *El Jarama* won the Nadal prize, Ferlosio was twenty-eight, yet he was one of the oldest of this group of writers. It therefore seemed legitimate to consider that, whatever the limitations of the novels published in Spain in the late fifties and early sixties, they were very encouraging beginnings for young writers learning their trade in difficult conditions, and that they represented a prelude to better things. The appearance, in 1962, of *Tiempo de silencio*, by Luis Martín Santos, further seemed to confirm that this was so. The subject of the novel was still the squalor and misery of Spanish life, but the brilliantly original presentation breaks completely with the convention of straightforward descriptive narrative. Reality is fragmented and re-created in a series of compelling visions, and the author's verbal and stylistic virtuosity is reminiscent of *Ulysses*. The novel exudes an artistic exuberance and self-confidence rarely to be met with in the sober documentary fiction of post-war Spain. Without ceasing to be an indictment of a grim and silent society, it is an exciting work of art of impressive imaginative scope. It also restores to Spanish prose fiction a traditional vein of grotesque satire, which seemed to have been in danger of disappearing.

Everything seemed to indicate that *Tiempo de silencio* was the transitional step for which the Spanish novel had been waiting. But in 1964 Martín Santos died in a car accident at the age of thirty-nine. Although it is improbable that the fate of the Spanish novel hung on the career of this one young writer, the fact is that after his death prose fiction relapsed into a puzzling failure of self-confidence. It was as if, after a decade or more of committed social realism, many novelists came to the conclusion that their commitment had had no social or political effect, and that their realism had restricted their development as literary artists. Some of the best of them—Ferlosio, Fernández Santos, Carmen Martín Gaite, Sueiro, Luis Goytisolo—gave up writing novels, at least for some years, and in some cases apparently for good. Ignacio Aldecoa, whose finely written novels and stories had a lyrical sensitivity which set them somewhat apart from those of his contemporaries, and which might have survived the waning of the vogue for social realism, died in 1969, only forty-four years old. Cela has continued to publish during the sixties, but his passion for self-advertisement and for originality at any price has led him increasingly into producing flippant trivia which neither match his earlier novels in quality nor help to substantiate his repeated claim that he is the most important living Spanish novelist.

The late sixties, then, have witnessed something of a pause in prose fiction, while writers have taken stock of their situation and essayed some tentative new directions. It is too soon to say which directions are likely to prove most fruitful, but at least it is clear that the wave of sober testimonial realism has spent itself, and that novelists are returning to the concept of fiction as an experimental art rather than a social duty. The change of outlook has had different effects on established novelists. On the older ones, like Cela and Delibes, it has not been propitious. Cela's reaction, to judge by his most recent novel, *San Camilo, 1936* (1969), has been to drag his feet, and to return to the atmosphere, if not the style, of *La colmena.* The new book looks back nauseously to the beginnings of the Civil War, with the apparent purpose of destroying anyone's pretensions that the conflict was between right and wrong. The technique, a kind of stream of consciousness in which prosaic reality and historical events are mingled with dream and myth, is potentially interesting, but the stream turns out to be mainly a river of filth and agony, chilling in its lack of compassion, and monotonous in its repetitious insistence on the sordid and petty. Cela's depressing and disgusting vision of this particular historical moment makes the book positively tendentious, but his choice of subject and his treatment are surprisingly old-fashioned for a novelist of such determined originality.

Delibes, on the other hand, has made a notable break with his usual type of novel in *Parábola del náufrago* (1969). Its theme is still one of despair at the way in which simple, humane values founder on the brutal efficiency of modern society, but Delibes now makes his familiar protest by means of an elaborate allegorical fantasy, more sharply satirical than is his custom, and peppered with irritating stylistic tricks whose purpose one must charitably suppose to be that of making mock of such tricks. *Parábola del náufrago* is an awkward compromise between Delibes's long-standing preoccupations and the changes which the Spanish novel is currently undergoing. In respect of the latter, perhaps the most significant feature of the book is that, although there are a few veiled allusions to specifically Spanish problems, Delibes's subject is not Spain, but the evils of modern paternalistic capitalism at large. Delibes would appear to share the present determination of a number of Spanish novelists to break out of their parochial introspection and address themselves to the world at large. A prominent and promising example of this determination is Daniel Sueiro's recent *Corte de corteza* (1969), also on the subject of the horrors of modern Western civilisation in general, but a great deal more incisive, witty, and readable than *Parábola del náufrago*.

Finally, mention must be made of a remarkable change in the writing of one of the best-known purveyors of the social realism of the fifties and sixties, Juan Goytisolo. Since his first novel, *Juegos de manos* (1954), Goytisolo has expressed his angry and pessimistic opinions of the state of Spain in a series of novels and essays which have got him into considerable trouble with the censor. But by the mid-sixties, like many of his contemporaries, his work was betraying signs of weariness and despair. In 1966, however, he took the important step of publishing *Señas de identidad*, an extremely thoughtful and moving view of the Twenty-Five Years of Peace, but also a highly original and imaginative literary artefact which has indisputably re-established Goytisolo as a very gifted writer who has weathered the crisis through which the Spanish novel has passed.

Unfortunately, the severely critical nature of his very personal account of contemporary Spain made it necessary for the novel to be published in Mexico, and has in all probability turned the author into a permanent exile. Indeed, his latest novel, *Reivindicación del Conde Don Julián* (1970), also published in Mexico, takes the theme of exile as its main subject. Both *Señas de identidad* and *Reivindicación del Conde Don Julián* are very fine novels, and in their imaginative scope and stylistic inventiveness they stand comparison with the best products of contemporary Spanish American fiction. Only the fact that the author of these two impressive books must now be considered a writer in exile deters one from supposing that the Spanish novel may be about to make substantial contributions to the literature of the world.

IV. POETRY

In terms of sheer quantity, the period since the Civil War has been a fruitful one for poetry in Spain. In an era which has been unfavourable to all the arts in many ways, it is possible that more poetry has been published and read than ever before—though this is not to suggest, of course, either that reading poetry has suddenly become a popular recreation in Spain, or that Spain can count on a wider public for poetry than can other countries. The oppressive atmosphere in post-war Spain may have contributed to this relative proliferation, for poetry can make its points more subtly than prose, and the Spanish censor often permits publication of potentially subversive work provided it is certain that it will have only a small circulation. Whatever the reasons, poetry has flourished, in the big cities and in the provinces, in poetry magazines, in anthologies, and in serial publications like the famous 'Colección Adonais'. It has also manifested considerable variety, and any attempt to summarise its tendencies must limit itself to very general characteristics if it is not to ignore cross-currents and changes of direction of real importance.

One indisputable characteristic, however, is what is frequently referred to as the 'rehumanización' of post-war poetry. The term is misleading in that it supposes a sharp contrast with an alleged 'deshumanización' during the pre-war period. But it does indicate a definite shift of emphasis away from the idea of the Poet as a special kind of person, a privileged visionary, a hypersensitive sufferer, or an exquisite aesthete. Post-war Spanish poets have asserted, either by implication or by direct statement, that they are not the guardians of any esoteric truth, but men and women like any others, and so impelled to speak of common, collective experience in clear, explicit terms which their fellow-men can understand. This impulse has often, though not always, meant poetry of social realism, political protest, or religious affirmation. It has also invariably reflected a clear sense of belonging to a particular time, place, and society. An acceptance of the importance of temporality has replaced the poetic search for essence and eternity. Not surprisingly, the influence of Antonio Machado's poetry during this period has been immense. His dictum that poetry is 'la palabra esencial en el tiempo' has become an article of faith; his 'testimonial' poetry on the subject of Spain has been read with admiration; and his strictures of what he considered the poetic tomfooleries of the twenties and thirties have been remembered with approval.

Although the contrast between poetry before and after the war is in many respects striking, the post-war poets did not reject the work of their immediate seniors on principle. The memories of Lorca and Hernández were revered, and the forbidden post-war works of exiled Spanish poets were read eagerly when they could be got. The Peruvian César Vallejo and the Chilean Pablo Neruda, whose cries of anguish and protest seemed to have anticipated the mood of much Spanish poetry after 1939, also exercised considerable influence on several poets. Vicente Aleixandre and Gerardo Diego were still in Spain, still highly respected, and if their post-war work followed rather than directed the current of Spanish poetry, it was still esteemed by many of the younger poets.

Another member of the Lorca–Guillén generation who remained in Spain was Dámaso Alonso (1898-   ). Alonso had been intimately associated with all the activities of that generation of poets, but most importantly in his capacity as a scholar and critic. His own poetic output had been small, and marginal to the achievements of his illustrious contemporaries. But in 1944 he published a historically important book of poetry, *Hijos de la ira*, a book to surprise those who thought him only an erudite, middle-aged professor. The poems pour out a torrent of rage, revulsion, and despair, expressed in long, tumbling lines of free verse and in a vocabulary of violence, ugliness, and rottenness. They contain no specific protest, either political, social, or metaphysical, but constitute a raucous cry of horror, inspired by the spectacle of the world as Alonso saw it in 1944, a spectacle which, as he has said, made him suddenly sick and tired of elegant aesthetic exercises.

The cry resounded loudly in what was until then a predominantly tranquil poetic atmosphere, and initiated what Alonso himself has described as the division of Spanish poetry into 'poesía arraigada' and 'poesía desarraigada'.[3] Not all poets of the period fit neatly into one or other of the categories, of course, but it is true that the same root-causes of most post-war Spanish poetry—anguish and despair—find expression in two distinctly different ways: either seeking refuge in traditional sources of consolation or raging against the dying of the light. The reappearance of God as a major subject of poetry has been a marked feature of the epoch, and emphasises the division. Some poets have appealed to Him, with varying degrees of hope, for comfort; others have cursed Him for His absence, indifference, and silence. Poets like Vivanco, Panero, Rosales, Muñoz Rojas, Ridruejo, and Valverde thank Him for His mercies in spite of everything. Celaya, Crémer, and Otero are more inclined either to make a cold note of His absence or to abuse Him for His irresponsibility. Between the two extremes, Bousoño, Vicente Gaos, and José Hidalgo ask Him difficult questions to which He does not reply.

Such differences of attitude tend to correspond to differences in poetic aims and manner. Vivanco, Rosales, Panero, and others like them began or resumed their poetic work after the war mainly with timid, formal exercises in pastoral, amorous, or religious poetry, proclaiming Garcilaso as their master. But later they turned increasingly to talking in a low, unpretentious tone of the common experience of everyday reality. The utterly commonplace commands their attention with almost embarrassing persistence. Vivanco finds God in a taxi. Rosales, in his best book, *La casa encendida* (1949), meditates, with simple sincerity and in plain language, on the immediate reality of everyday life. Rafael Morales addresses a sonnet to a dustbin—not from any desire to shock or disgust, but simply as an honest attempt to make a poem, as the last line says, out of 'el llanto de lo humilde y lo olvidado'. The modesty of this kind of poetry, its resignation to a drab reality, and its capacity for finding the world well made, are quite extraordinary. Perhaps such qualities deserve respect, but they make for a poetic art which seems to wish to renounce most of the achievements of which poetry is capable. Its concern with the here and now is extremely limiting. When Rosales addresses God in the supremely unpoetic line: 'pero quiero pedirte, de algún modo, que no derribes aún aquella casa de La Coruña', he is certainly situated in a very precise moment in time, and as far removed from abstract essences as anyone could wish to be. But this is not Machado's temporality either, in spite of its mild concern with time's destructive effects. Machado was preoccupied with the flux of time in the sense of the coexistence of past, present, and future in personal consciousness; when he wrote about everyday life it was with a strong awareness of the significance of the historical moment. Both kinds of temporality tend to be absent from the personal, anecdotal, or descriptive poems of writers like Panero and Rosales.

A sense of historical moment is by no means absent, however, from all Spanish poetry of the last thirty years. Much of the work of poets like Gabriel Celaya, Victoriano Crémer, Blas de Otero, Eugenio de Nora, and José Hierro springs directly, like *Hijos de la ira*, from a painful awareness of historical circumstances. A good deal of it is social or political protest. In 1952, Celaya said that he regarded poetry as 'un instrumento, entre otros, para transformer el mundo'.[4] Hierro has modestly stated that the only enduring value of his own poetry will be its documentary significance.[5] Like some of the novelists of this period, but rather earlier, these poets saw it as their clear duty to renounce aesthetic considerations in order to break the silence and denounce injustice in clear, angry tones and often in plain, prosaic language.

But, also like the novelists, they have grown disillusioned with their efforts. Their poems have not transformed the world, and in most cases, however disposed one may be to respect their aim of bringing poetry out of supposed esoteric obscurity and into the market-place, the results have not been happy ones for their art. For all the emphasis on reality and immediacy, much of this social poetry has an awkwardly abstract air, and is less firmly rooted in real, personal experience than that of Rosales or Panero. And the old, basic problem of utilitarian, didactic poetry remains: if the purpose is to speak plainly to a wide audience, why not write in prose? As has been suggested, a partial and topical answer in the fifties may have been the matter of censorship, but it is an answer that does nothing to solve the problem, as many of the poets themselves seem to have realised. Fortunately it is not necessary to judge Spanish poetry since the war purely as an instrument of social and political protest. Although all the poets whose names are commonly associated with 'poesía social' have written their share of prosaic testimonial poetry, the best of them cannot be summed up and dismissed as writers who have tried to do their social duty at the expense of their art. Some of their poetry will survive for the reasons poetry usually survives—that it is well written, and communicates insights which are emotionally and intellectually satisfying or enlightening. Celaya, for instance, whose aim was once to speak of contemporary problems in a plain manner, and who entitled one of his early volumes *Tranquilamente hablando* (1947) to emphasise its unadorned, conversational style, in fact often injects his poetry with lyrical passion and power. He is also a poet of many moods. Among his harsh cries of revolt there are radiant interludes which celebrate the pleasure of simply being alive. He is less impressive when he writes on large abstractions—Spain, poetry—than when he descends to more specific elements of experience, as he does in his moving 'Carta a Andrés Basterra' (*Las cartas boca arriba*, 1951). Otero, too, wanted to speak forthrightly to men in fields and factories, but is often distracted from this purpose by an irrepressibly original creative imagination and a cultivated taste for metaphor which make him, as his political and social views do not, one of the most forceful and attractive poets of contemporary Spain. Hierro, always more of a personal than a social poet, can combine intimate feeling with an assured mastery of the poet's craft. In spite of his prognostication, it is likely that if he is read by future generations it will not be for documentary reasons, but because he knows how to organise the expression of unchanging human sentiments in controlled and illuminating poetic form.

The vogue for poetry of social testimony has waned markedly during the sixties. This has had the healthy effect of consigning a crowd of very minor poets to obscurity and emphasising the enduring excellence of others. The most recent work of Celaya, Otero, and Hierro is at least as good as anything they did in the fifties, and increasingly suggests that poetry for them is now a means of exploring personal experience rather than of representing a historical and social reality. In fact this idea of poetry never disappeared entirely after the war. Such poets as Vicente Gaos and Carlo Bousoño have consistently used their art to investigate, with all the earnestness of a Salinas or a Cernuda, their own feelings, aspirations, and fears, and to meditate on what they find enigmatic in their own existence and in their manner of apprehending outer reality. Theirs is serious, thoughtful poetry, though it is for the most part, and particularly in

Bousoño's case, extremely nebulous, dealing characteristically in abstractions and in vague apprehensions repeatedly undermined by doubt. When these characteristics are less prominent, when Bousoño, for instance, anchors his meditations more firmly in a particular experience or object, an actual landscape, an old door in the Plaza Mayor of Madrid, there is a notable gain in fine analytic perceptions.

In the historical perspective this kind of poetry is beginning to acquire—Bousoño has been publishing poems since 1945—it seems, after all, to belong to the mainstream of the evolution of Spanish poetry during this century, while the commonplace of the Vivanco–Rosales–Panero school and the rebellious testimony of the social poets appear as momentary deviations. Younger poets are continuing to treat poetry as a subtle instrument of understanding, and are no more concerned than is Bousoño that what it communicates should be simple and immediately intelligible to all kinds of reader. The verses of one of the best of the younger poets, José Ángel Valente, which apply a clear intelligence to complex feelings, proclaim what he has often affirmed directly: that for him, making a poem is a concluding stage in understanding his own experience. Having made the poem, he then hopes that his experience will be meaningful for others as a result of his attempt to find the right words in which to express it. Such a classic concept of poetry clearly marks no departure from the central tradition of the art in twentieth-century Spain. Spanish poets from Machado and Jiménez to Guillén and Alberti would have had no quarrel with it.

Such a concept would also appear to be the one underlying the work of the most accomplished young poets in Spain today, poets like Francisco Brines, Claudio Rodríguez, and Carlos Sahagún. Their poetry bears the mark of its age in that it adopts an unpretentious, absolutely unrhetorical style, and deals with common experience rather than with rare visions of eternal truths; but it also rises boldly and imaginatively to the challenge of poetry's capacity for exploring experience in a freer, subtler way than prose. As far as one can tell at the moment, the prospects for Spanish poetry are good. The younger poets are certainly not the products of any passing fashion. They are not isolated from other European poetry—Valente, Rodríguez, and Sahagún have followed the tradition of Salinas, Guillén, and Cernuda in spending some time teaching in foreign universities—and they are familiar with the currents of Spanish poetry which were momentarily interrupted by the Civil War.

Furthermore, they seem to have come to terms with the fact that serious poetry in modern times can only have a very limited audience. This may be a pity, but it is also an inescapable fact, and the survival of poetry of any worthwhile kind depends on its being recognised as such.

V. DRAMA

The last thirty years have been among the dreariest in the history of the Spanish stage. In addition to the difficulties which have beset poetry and the novel during this period, any attempt at serious drama has had to contend with the reappearance of all the traditional obstacles of the pre-war theatrical era. In reality they had never disappeared; but there had been a time, during the favourable atmosphere of the Republic, when it seemed that Lorca, Alberti, Hernández, Casona, and Jardiel Poncela were presenting a challenge that threatened to change the course of modern Spanish theatrical history. With Lorca dead, Hernández dying in gaol, Alberti and Casona in exile, however, the first few years after the Civil War produced a great quantity of plays of unimaginably wretched quality which nevertheless won the applause of large audiences who were determined to forget the Civil War, the World War, the atom bomb, and the desperate state of Spain. The only minor reliefs from this degrading spectacle were productions of plays from the traditional repertoire of the Spanish theatre, and of some translations of foreign works—generally put on in the two state-subsidised theatres, El Español and María Guerrero—and the tired, ever more reactionary, but still competent dramas of Jacinto Benavente.

In the late forties and early fifties the situation improved slightly, but for the most part only in the sense that more dexterous writers put together better brands of escapist triviality for the entertainment of the all-powerful middle-class audiences. Writers like Edgar Neville, J. López Rubio, and V. Ruiz Iriarte have worked conscientiously and successfully to the principle that a play should give the public exactly what it wants, and that what it wants is something that recognisably reflects the real world, but in a way that makes it more attractive or amusing than it really is. Another minor school, composed of Miguel Mihura and his fellow-collaborators from the early days of the famous satirical magazine *La Codorniz*, have chosen to make their plays out of absurd and surprising jokes about life, often stylishly amusing, but always taking care never to step over the line which separates such jokes from a potentially tragic sense of the absurdity of human existence.

In addition to such dramatists who have pursued the modest aim of trying to make an honest living out of writing for the commercial stage, there have been some writers who have continued to make their art a matter of personal or social conscience. Inevitably such writers have had to contend with the tastes and outlook of the kind of Spaniard who can habitually afford the price of a theatre ticket. Some dramatists' preoccupations have coincided nearly enough with those of their typical audience for their work to have been successful on the stage. A notable example is J. Calvo Sotelo, whose plays have examined serious matters from a sincerely committed Catholic bourgeois standpoint. Like Miguel Delibes, Calvo Sotelo is prepared to bite the hand that feeds him, and to chastise his own sort for their hypocrisy, greed, and indifference to questions of conscience. His most famous play, *La muralla* (1954), provoked considerable controversy in its day, but it was also a great success in the theatre. As with all drama of social conscience produced in Spain in the twentieth century, one cannot help thinking that if the typical theatre-going public applauds it, then it cannot be of any great social significance.

The same suspicions attend the work of a much more able and serious dramatist, Antonio Buero Vallejo (1916-)—suspicions not relating to artistic achievement, which is by any standards much greater than Calvo Sotelo's, but to the social theses of his works. In Buero Vallejo's case it is particularly necessary to make such an observation: his war service on the Republican side, his consequent imprisonment after the war, and the fact that some of his plays are set in a contemporary Spanish context which acknowledges the existence of poverty and hardship, have caused some critics to exaggerate the social-realist testimony and polemical purpose of his work. His first successful play, *Historia de una escalera* (1949), won an important literary prize, and was so well received by the public that the traditional annual performance of *Don Juan Tenorio* in the Teatro Español was cancelled so that its run could continue. But by any standards other than those of the Spanish theatre of the time, *Historia de una escalera* is a tedious, clumsy play which laboriously unfolds a dull sequence of events in the lives of the tenants of a poor block of flats, and demonstrates that human aspirations to happiness are often frustrated by circumstances and disappointed with the passage of time. But in spite of the very trite message, Buero's treatment of the theme is both serious and easy to follow, and the realism of the play's setting and language gave it a certain vigour which distinguished it sharply from the anaemic artifice of its rivals on the Spanish stage of 1949. Since then Buero Vallejo has revealed that he has the confidence and ability to vary his style as he pleases. Although his basic subject has continued to be man's quest for happiness and the various kinds of obstacle which block his path towards it, he has treated the theme in a quite impressively different series of manners —symbolic in plays like *En la ardiente oscuridad* (1950), *La señal que se espera* (1952), and *El concierto de San Ovidio* (1963), fantastic in *Irene o el tesoro* (1954), mythical in *La tejedora de sueños* (1952), and historical and social in *Un soñador para un pueblo* (1958) and *Las meninas* (1960). In *Hoy es fiesta* (1956), he returns to the impoverished Madrid scene of *Historia de una escalera,* but again without any marked social intent, for the play is a melodramatic tapestry of varieties of human experience in a humble setting, and has no distinctly polemical intention.

Buero Vallejo is certainly the ablest dramatist writing in Spain today. His latest play, *El sueño de la razón* (1970), is at least as good as anything he has written. But he is something of an isolated phenomenon. Although many of his plays have been successful in the theatre, they enjoy nothing like the popularity of the lightweight comedies of a writer like the incredibly prolific Alfonso Paso. On the other hand, Buero has attracted the criticism of more militant young writers for his lack of clear commitment to the social struggle and for his commercial success. His plays are not great drama, and it is hard to imagine that they would interest audiences in other countries. Nevertheless, his achievement has been considerable, for he has restored some seriousness and dignity to the Spanish theatre, and has persuaded the public to watch plays that deal honestly and intelligently with real problems.

The most interesting playwright among Buero's younger critics is Alfonso Sastre (1926-   ), who is deeply committed to drama of testimony and protest, and has therefore had a hard time of it with the censor. Most of his work is known only to those who have read it, or have seen it performed by private, usually student, groups. In fact, few of his plays deal with specifically Spanish problems, even when they are set in Spain; but this has not stopped them dividing Spanish attitudes into inflexible disapproval and fervent enthusiasm. Sastre's constant theme is oppression—by fear, force, wealth, or any other means—and the prospect of a real social revolution in our time. Although Sastre naturally regards such a prospect with hope, he also pays due regard to the dangers and moral problems it may present. He describes his work as realistic, but not photographically so. In fact it is realistic only in a very relative sense, frequently set in imaginary countries at imprecisely specified historical moments. His first notable success, *Escuadra hacia la muerte* (1953), takes place during the third world war. When his scene is contemporary Spain, his concern with local problems is only incidental. *Muerte en el barrio* (1956), for instance, was banned by the censor because it tells how the irresponsibility of a Spanish doctor leads to the death of a working-class child; but it is not an indictment of the Spanish health service so much as a worried look at a problem inherent in any system of social medicine. At a deeper level it also thoughtfully examines a theme of crime and punishment.

Sastre's plays make no secret of where he stands politically, and they are certainly aimed at 'transforming the world', not at providing entertainment or making money. Their purpose is moral inquiry, into problems about which Sastre feels deeply and which he investigates imaginatively. He holds the view, as did Unamuno and other pre-war dramatists, that Spanish drama lacks real tragedy, and among his own plays he personally prefers the most tragic ones—in addition to the two mentioned, *El cubo de la basura* (1965; written 1952), *Tierra roja* (1958), and *Guillermo Tell tiene los ojos tristes* (1955), the last being a novel version of the Swiss legend, in which Tell kills his son, as Sastre thinks the legend ought to say.

Sastre has written a great deal, and in spite of his variations of manner, his work suffers from repetitiousness of themes. This, together with a tendency towards excessive schematisation of plot— in the sense that the characters work out the message with the precision of automata—makes his plays rather predictable. But Sastre and Buero Vallejo are certainly the best two playwrights of the post-war period. Buero is the superior dramatic craftsman, but Sastre's work has a more outward-looking, European style than Buero's.

Other social drama in Spain has been disappointing. *La camisa* (1961) by Lauro Olmo, seemed a promising beginning from a young writer. It deals with the misery of life in a poor quarter of Madrid, pulling only such punches as the censor would have stopped, and making some telling and penetrating observations about the reality of poverty. But Olmo has not followed up his early promise. He now seems to be more interested in the novel than the theatre, and his recent play, *English spoken* (1968), is a thin and forced contrivance lacking the authenticity of *La camisa.*

As with poetry and the novel, the impetus has gone out of social literature, but, unlike the other genres, the theatre does not seem to have found anything to replace it. Bright new stars are hailed periodically, but at the moment no young dramatist has established himself sufficiently to show any sign of challenging the pre-eminence of Buero Vallejo, still less of interesting a foreign public. The commercial theatre thrives on a staple diet of soothingly orthodox bourgeois entertainment produced by a group of writers who know very well what they are doing and are happy in their work. In short, if the Spanish theatre is in a better state now than it was twenty years ago, it is because it could hardly be in a worse one; the immediate outlook, it must be admitted, is not favourable.

In recent years the Theatre of the Absurd has made its appearance in Spain. Its outstanding exponent is Fernando Arrabal (1932-   ). His works, whose debt to Beckett is manifest, include *El triciclo* (1953) and *Fando y Lis* (1962). Arrabal has chosen to live in France. So far most of his works have appeared only in French translation.

NOTES

1. F. Ayala, *Mis páginas mejores* (Madrid, 1965), p. 19.
2. E. C. Riley, 'Sobre el arte de Sánchez Ferlosio: aspectos de *El Jarama*', *De Filología* (Buenos Aires), Año IX (1963), 201-21.
3. D. Alonso, *Poetas españoles contemporáneos* (Madrid, 1958), p. 366-80.
4. *Antología consultada de la joven poesía española* (Santander, 1952), p. 44.
5. Ibid, p. 107.

BIBLIOGRAPHY

Introduction
R. Carr, *Spain, 1808-1939* (Oxford, 1966)

Chapter 1
C. Barja, *Libros y autores contemporáneos* (Madrid, 1935)
E. G. de Nora, *La novela española contemporánea* (Madrid, 1958-62)
E. Salcedo, *Vida de don Miguel* (Salamanca, 1964)
J. Marías, *Miguel de Unamuno* (Madrid, 1943)
A. Sánchez Barbudo, *Estudios sobre Unamuno y Machado* (Madrid, 1959)
C. Blanco Aguinaga, *El Unamuno contemplativo* (Mexico, 1959)
J. Rubia Barcia, M. A. Zeitlin (eds.), *Unamuno, Creator and Creation* (Berkeley and Los Angeles, 1967)
Cuadernos de la Cátedra de Miguel de Unamuno (Salamanca, 1954-   )
G. Díaz Plaja, *Las estéticas de Valle-Inclán* (Madrid, 1965)
A. Risco, *La estética de Valle-Inclán* (Madrid, 1966)
A. Zahareas, S. Greenfield (eds.), *Ramón del Valle-Inclán. An Appraisal of his Life and Works* (New York, 1968)
Revista de Occidente, 44-45 (Nov.-Dec. 1966), Homenaje a Valle-Inclán
R. Gullón (ed.), *Valle-Inclán Centennial Studies* (Austin, Texas, 1968)
F. Baeza, *Baroja y su mundo* (Madrid, 1961)
L. S. Granjel, *Retrato de Pío Baroja* (Barcelona, 1954)
J. Alberich, *Los ingleses y otros temas de Pío Baroja* (Madrid, 1966)
Revista de Occidente, 62 (May 1968), Homenaje a Pío Baroja
N. Urrutia, *De Troteras a Tigre Juan* (Madrid, 1960)
M. Baquero Goyanes, *Perspectivismo y contraste* (Madrid, 1963), pp. 161-244
R. Vidal, *Gabriel Miró. Le Style et les moyens d'expression* (Bordeaux, 1964)

V. Ramos, *Vida y obra de Gabriel Miró* (Madrid, 1955)

J. Guillén, 'Adequate Language: Gabriel Miró', in *Language and Poetry* (Cambridge, Mass., 1961)

L. J. Woodward, 'Les images et leur function dans *Nuestro Padre San Daniel* de Gabriel Miró', *BH*, 56 (1954), 110-32

A. Krause, *The Little Philosopher* (Berkeley and Los Angeles, 1948)

M. Granell, *Estética de Azorín* (Madrid, 1958)

L. S. Granjel, *Retrato de Azorín* (Madrid, 1958)

J. M. Martínez Cachero, *Las novelas de Azorín* (Madrid, 1960)

L. Livingstone, 'The Pursuit of Form in the Novels of *Azorín*', *PMLA*, 77 (1962)

E. Inman Fox, introduction to Azorín, *La voluntad* (Madrid, 1968)

Cuadernos Hispanoamericanos, 226-227 (1968)

L. S. Granjel, *Retrato de Ramón* (Madrid, 1963)

G. Gómez de la Serna, *Ramón. Obra y vida* (Madrid, 1963)

Chapter 2

G. Diego (ed.), *Poesía española contemporánea (1901-1934). Antología.* Nueva edición completa (Madrid, 1959)

J. L. Cano, *Poesía española del siglo XX* (Madrid, 1960)

L. Cernuda, *Estudios sobre poesía española contemporánea* (Madrid, 1957)

L. F. Vivanco, *Introducción a la poesía española contemporánea* (Madrid, 1957)

C. Zardoya, *Poesía española contemporánea* (Madrid, 1961)

——, *Poesía del 98 y del 27* (Madrid, 1968)

D. Alonso, *Poetas españoles contemporáneos* (Madrid, 1958)

R. Gullón, *Direcciones del modernismo* (Madrid, 1963)

G. Brotherston, *Manuel Machado. A Reappraisal* (Cambridge, 1968)

H. T. Young, *The Victorious Expression. A Study of Four Contemporary Spanish Poets* (Unamuno, A. Machado, Jiménez, Lorca) (Madison, Wisconsin, 1964)

A. Sánchez Barbudo, *La poesía de Antonio Machado* (Barcelona, 1967)

R. de Zubiria, *La poesía de Antonio Machado* (Madrid, 1955)

E. Neddermann, *Die symbolistischen Stilemente in Werke von Juan Ramón Jiménez* (Hamburg, 1935)

S. Ulibarri, *El mundo poético de Juan Ramón Jiménez* (Madrid, 1962)

L. R. Cole, *The Religious Instinct in the Poetry of Juan Ramón Jiménez* (Oxford, 1967)

P. R. Olson, *Circle of Paradox. Time and Essence in the Poetry of Juan Ramón Jiménez* (Baltimore, 1967)

A. Sánchez Barbudo, *La segunda época de Juan Ramón Jiménez* (Madrid, 1962)

G. de Torre, *Historia de las literaturas de vanguardia* (Madrid, 1965)

G. Videla, *El ultraísmo* (Madrid, 1963)

J. González Muela, J. M. Rozas, *La generación poética de 1927. Estudio, antología y documentación* (Madrid, 1966)

J. Guillén, 'The Language of the Poem. One Generation', in *Language and Poetry* (Cambridge, Mass., 1961)

C. B. Morris, *A Generation of Spanish Poets, 1920-1936* (Cambridge, 1969)

E. Dehennin, *Le résurgence de Góngora et la génération poétique de 1927* (Paris, 1962)

M. Laffranque, *Les idées esthétiques de Federico García Lorca* (Paris, 1967)

J. M. Aguirre, 'El sonambulismo de Federico García Lorca', *BHS*, XLIV (1967), 267-85.

Á. del Río, '*Poet in New York*: Twenty-five Years After', in F. G. Lorca, *Poet in New York* (London, 1955)

L. Spitzer, 'El conceptismo interior de Pedro Salinas', in *Lingüística e historia literaria* (Madrid, 1955)

C. Feal Deibe, *La poesía de Pedro Salinas* (Madrid, 1965)

Á. del Río, 'El poeta Pedro Salinas: vida y obra', in *Estudios sobre literatura contemporánea española* (Madrid, 1966)

Alma de Zubizarreta, *Pedro Salinas; el diálogo creador* (Madrid, 1969)

R. Gullón y J. M. Blecua, *La poesía de Jorge Guillén (dos ensayos)* (Zaragoza, 1949)

J. Casalduero, *Cántico de Jorge Guillén* (Madrid, 1953)

P. Darmangeat, *Jorge Guillén ou le cantique émerveillé* (Paris, 1958)

J. González Muela, *La realidad y Jorge Guillén* (Madrid, 1962)

Luminous Reality. The Poetry of Jorge Guillén (Norman, Okla., 1969)

C. Bousoño, *La poesía de Vicente Aleixandre* (Madrid, 1956)

C. B. Morris, *Rafael Alberti's 'Sobre los ángeles': Four Major Themes* (Hull, 1966)

S. Salinas de Marichal, *El mundo poético de Rafael Alberti* (Madrid, 1968)

P. W. Silver, '*Et in Arcadia Ego*'. *A Study of the Poetry of Luis Cernuda* (London, 1965)

A. Coleman, *Other Voices: A Study of the Late Poetry of Luis Cernuda* (Chapel Hill, 1969)

La Caña Gris (Valencia), 6-8 (1962). Homenaje a Luis Cernuda

C. Blanco Aguinaga, *Emilio Prados: Vida y obra* (New York, 1960)

J. Cano Ballesta, *La poesía de Miguel Hernández* (Madrid, 1962)

Chapter 3

A. Valbuena Prat, *Historia del teatro español* (Barcelona, 1956)
G. Torrente Ballester, *Teatro español contemporáneo* (2nd edn., Madrid, 1968)
R. Pérez de Ayala, *Las máscaras* (4th edn., Buenos Aires, 1948)
F. Ruiz Ramón, *Historia del teatro español,* II: Siglo XX (Madrid, 1971)

Chapter 4

J. R. Marra-López, *Narrativa española fuera de España, 1939-1961* (Madrid, 1963)
J. Chabás, *Literatura española contemporánea: 1898-1950* (Havana, 1952)
F. Carrasquer, *'Imán' y la novela histórica de Ramón J. Sender* (Zaandijk, Holland, 1968)
M. S. Peñuelas, *Conversaciones con Ramón J. Sender* (Madrid, 1969)
S. H. Eoff, 'The Challenge of Absurdity', in *The Modern Spanish Novel* (London, 1962)
K. Ellis, *El arte narrativo de Francisco de Ayala* (Madrid, 1964)
P. Ilie, *La novelística de Camilo José Cela* (Madrid, 1963)
A. Zamora Vicente, *Camilo José Cela* (Madrid, 1962)
J. L. Alborg, *Hora actual de la novela española* (Madrid, 1958-62)
A. Iglesias Laguna, *Treinta años de novela española: 1938-1968* (Madrid, 1969)
J. M. Castellet, *Un cuarto de siglo de poesía española (1939-1964)* (Barcelona, 1966)
David Bary, 'Sobre el nombrar poético en la poesía española contemporánea', *PSA*, CXXXI (1967)

INDEX

Printed in Great Britain by
The Garden City Press Limited, Letchworth, Hertfordshire, SG6 1JS